ATLAS OF

HUMAN
ANATOMY

ATLAS OF
HUMAN
ANATOMY

FRANZ FROHSE
Late of the University of Berlin

MAX BRÖDEL
Late of Johns Hopkins University

LEON SCHLOSSBERG
Johns Hopkins University

*Sixth Edition (1961): Text by SAMUEL SMITH,
Edited by M. F. ASHLEY MONTAGU and ERNEST
F. KERBY; Section on Endocrine Glands by
CHARLES F. GESCHICKTER, Illustrated by LEON
SCHLOSSBERG; Notes by JESSE F. WILLIAMS;
Complete Summaries and Up-to-Date Terminology*

BARNES & NOBLE BOOKS

A DIVISION OF HARPER & ROW, PUBLISHERS

New York, Hagerstown, San Francisco, London

Many of the colored illustrations in this book are miniature reproductions of the wall-size charts published by A. J. Nystrom & Company, 3333 Elston Avenue, Chicago, Illinois. Write to them for complete information.

Sixth Edition, 1961

L. C. catalogue card number 61-15471

Hardbound Edition SBN 389 02199 7
Paperback Edition SBN 389 00015 9

79 80   12 11 10 9

PREFACE

This new edition of the Atlas of Human Anatomy provides in pocket size: (1) a complete and perfectly reproduced set of the Frohse-Brödel wall charts; (2) Leon Schlossberg's equally expert supplementary charts; (3) an explanatory text written by Dr. Samuel Smith and edited by Dr. Ashley Montagu and Dr. Ernest F. Kerby; (4) ten special color charts of the endocrine system; (5) twenty-two scale drawings showing enlarged microscopic sections—their cells and blood vessels; (6) explanatory notes by Dr. Jesse F. Williams; (7) a description of the endocrine glands by Charles F. Geschickter, M.D., edited by Dr. Ernest F. Kerby; and (8) numerous line drawings (some prepared by G. H. Lahr, others by Albert Janson) taken from E. B. Steen and M. F. Ashley Montagu, *Anatomy and Physiology* (2 vols. in the College Outline Series)

For convenient reference the nomenclatures appear on the same pages as the charts. The terms used throughout the text and chart sections incorporate many of the changes approved at the most recent International Congress of Anatomists.

For many years the admirable illustrations appealed to large diversified audiences, beginning with the first reproduction in America (before World War I) of the large-sized charts prepared by Professor Franz Frohse, of the University of Berlin. Additional charts, including those of the circulatory system, throat, heart, neck, and male and female genito-urinary organs, were constructed by Professor Max Brödel, of the Johns Hopkins Medical School. After arrangements for publication of these charts in book form had been made, several further modifications seemed advisable. At that time Mr. Leon Schlossberg constructed the supplementary charts. These included two illustrations of the head: one showing the base of the skull, the other showing the base of the brain; and a new figure to illustrate the vascular system of the brain. The latter figure (on page 128) amplifies and refines the data shown (on page 125) at the upper terminus of Professor Frohse's Schema of Circulation.

In addition to the comprehensive text, many of the charts are accompanied by brief explanatory notes written by Dr. Jesse Feiring Williams, Professor Emeritus, of Columbia University. These notes supplement both the text and the remarkable colored illustrations so that the reader can readily grasp the essential principles applicable to the visual details.

For the section on endocrine glands a general chart was prepared by Mr. Schlossberg, assisted by investigators in the Johns Hopkins Medical School. His chart (on page 146), which shows gross anatomy of the head and trunk, functions principally in providing a topographic base for locating the endocrines. Illustrations of the latter are necessarily microscopic in character: there are low-power photographs which make relationships and details stand out clearly; and, in juxtaposition to these, there are other reproductions which show portions of the same fields in higher magnification.

Anatomy (from the Greek *anatemnein*, to cut up) is the scientific study of the structure of living things. Human anatomy is that division of anatomy which studies the human body as a whole and also each of its parts. Few, indeed, are the scholars who possess a detailed knowledge of human anatomy, which is so complex that even professional anatomists specialize on one or a few structures while acquiring only a working knowledge of the others. It is not too difficult, however, to master the basic principles of the subject, and the time and effort devoted to this task will be most worth-while. The study of anatomy not only is essential for the student of medicine and allied sciences, but also is useful for the layman interested in understanding the facts of organic life. The Atlas of Human Anatomy, in its present new edition, should meet the needs of both the medical practitioner and the layman for a brief text and a convenient reference work in this important science.

CONTENTS

ATLAS OF
HUMAN
ANATOMY

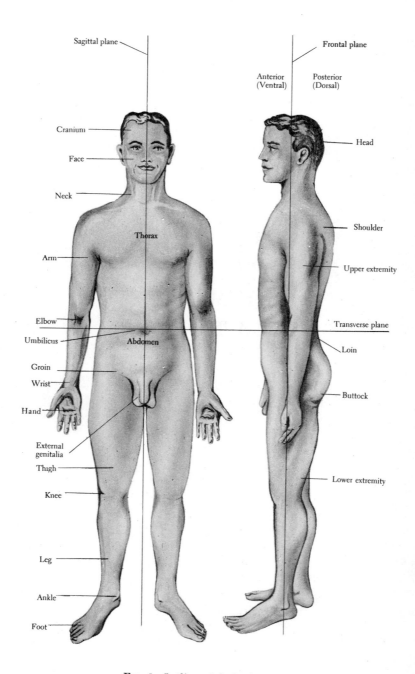

FIG. 1. Outline of body in anatomic position.

I—INTRODUCTION

The science of human anatomy describes the structure of the body and its parts The two principal methods of this science are called *gross anatomy* and *histology*. In gross anatomy the dissected body and its parts are observed by the unaided eye. In histology the tissues and organs are examined with the aid of a microscope.

Anatomy has a number of branches. In *developmental anatomy* the growth and development of the body are analyzed. This branch includes a subdivision, *embryology*, which studies the prenatal growth of the organism. *Genetics* deals with the mechanisms of heredity; *dermatology*, with the skin; *osteology*, with the skeletal system; *myology*, with the muscles; *neurology*, with the nervous system; *angiology*, with the heart and circulatory system; *splanchnology*, with the internal organs of respiration, digestion, elimination, and reproduction; and *endocrinology*, with the endocrine glands.

TERMINOLOGY

Scientific terms used by anatomists make information about the body definite and precise. The terms in this book have been brought up to date, in accordance with the decisions of the recent (Sixth) International Congress of Anatomists. One can readily identify many of these terms by referring to the accompanying illustrations. But it will be helpful to bear in mind the following terms denoting the locations of organs or parts of the body: anterior (toward the front); posterior (toward the back); superior (upper); inferior (lower); ventral (toward the anterior side); dorsal (toward the posterior side); superficial (on or near the surface); deep (distant from the surface); proximal (nearest to the beginning or to the point of attachment); and distal (farthest from a stated point or from a point of attachment). The standard anatomic position is the erect position, with the arms at the sides, palms facing forward.

The following terms denote sections or planes of the body: sagittal (a cut divides the body into right and left portions); midsagittal (a cut divides the body into right and left halves);

transverse or cross section (a cut divides the body into upper and lower portions); and coronal or frontal (a cut divides the body into anterior and posterior portions).

PLAN OF THE BODY

Figure 1 shows the five regions of the body: the head, neck (cervical region), chest (thorax), abdomen, and limbs.

The body resembles a system of tubes within tubes. The body wall constitutes the outer tubes, consisting of the skin (integument), underlying tissues or fascia, muscles and bones, inner lining (pleura) of the chest, and inner lining (peritoneum) of the abdomino-pelvic cavity. Within this large cavity are the inner tubes (the digestive tract, including the liver, gallbladder, stomach, pancreas, intestines, and spleen; and the reproductive organs, sigmoid colon, and rectum). Note in Figure 2 the chest cavity containing the lungs, heart, trachea, and esophagus; the cranial cavity; and the dorsal (spinal) cavity. The body cavity (coelom) thus consists of four cavities containing the internal organs.

The skin shields the individual from his environment. The muscles and bones (with their connective tissues) provide motion and rigidity. At the back, the skull and backbone (vertebral column) house the central nervous system (the brain and spinal cord). In the front, the skull provides space for the major sense organs as well as for the nose and mouth which are the beginnings of the air passages (respiratory tract) and of the digestive tract (alimentary canal). The neck contains the gullet (esophagus)—as a continuation of the digestive tract—and the windpipe (trachea). The entrance to the trachea is formed by the voice box (larynx) for the production of speech. From the neck the passages lead into the largest segment of the body—into the cavities of the chest, abdomen, and pelvis. The chest and abdomen are separated by the diaphragm. The chest contains the lungs, as the terminus of the respiratory tract; the esophagus as a continuation of the alimentary tract; and the heart as the power center of the circulatory system of tubes (arteries and veins). Below the diaphragm the abdominal and pelvic cavities provide an undivided space for the remainder of the digestive tract and for the reproductive and urinary systems of tubes.

The chest surgeon's knife cutting into the middle of the chest

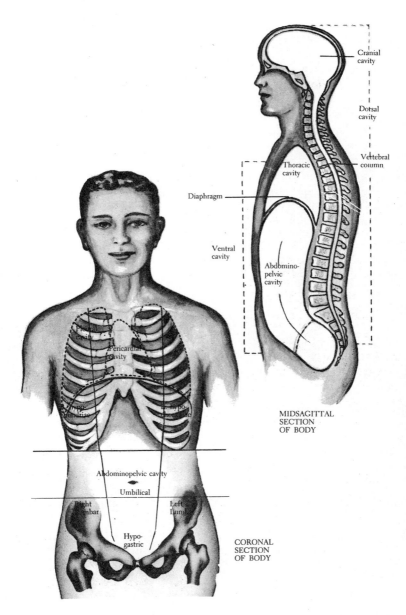

FIG. 2. Planes and sections of the body.

passes through skin, subcutaneous tissues, and layers of muscles, then encounters the chest cage which is formed by the breastbone (sternum) in front and the thoracic part of the spinal column toward the back. These two portions of the chest cage are joined together by the curving ribs and the muscles (intercostal muscles) between the ribs. To operate on the heart or lungs, the chest surgeon penetrates beyond the chest wall by removing segments of ribs or by spreading them apart. Similarly, an abdominal surgeon, after incising the skin and subcutaneous tissues of the abdominal wall, separates the deeper muscles along their grain and cuts through the inside lining (peritoneum) of the abdominal cavity, thus reaching the affected organ—such as, for example, an inflamed appendix.

BASIC LIFE PROCESSES

All living things are composed of cells, which consist of protoplasm, a complex, jelly-like material identified by Max Schulte in 1861 as the living substance in plants and animals.

Protoplasm is a colloidal mass of inorganic salts, water, and organic elements (proteins, carbohydrates, and fats). Rigorous investigations have failed to disclose in protoplasm any element which is not also found in nonliving substances. The vital character of protoplasm is therefore attributed, not to its constituents as such, but rather to their special arrangement and organization.

All the cells of the human body, like those of any living organism, exhibit the characteristics of irritability, conductivity, contractility, metabolism, reproduction, integration, and adaptation. *Irritability* refers to the power to react to a stimulus, which may be a mechanical, chemical, electrical, thermal, or photic force. *Conductivity* refers to the power to conduct impulses from one point to another; the cells in nerve tissue have an extremely high power of conductivity. *Contractility* refers to the power to contract and relax in order to move; the cells in muscle tissue have an extremely high power of contractility. *Metabolism* is a twofold process of (1) building protoplasm out of food—for cell growth and repair, and (2) breaking food down into simpler substances—for liberation of energy. *Reproduction* refers to the fact that living cells have power to repair and reproduce themselves. Each cell has a nucleus which splits into two equal parts, and the cell body divides into two separate

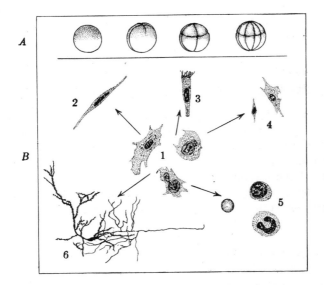

Fig. 3. The top row, *A*, shows, in diagram, the segmentation of a cell to produce a many-celled mass. Part *B* shows three embryonal cells (in center) and the arrows point to types into which they have differentiated. The specialization in function is also indicated. 1—cells with a common form able to carry on in a limited way all functions; 2—muscle cell (contraction); 3—epithelial cell (secretion); 4—connective cell (binds together and supports other parts); 5—blood cells (transport oxygen and protect the organism); and 6—nerve cell (responding to and sending impulses).

daughter cells resembling the mother cell. *Integration* refers to the power to coordinate, speed up, or inhibit activities so that they work together effectively; cells in the brain and other organs of the nervous system are extremely active in integration. *Adaptation* refers to the power of an organism to redirect its activities in response to the external environment.

The cells of the human body, originally very similar, differentiate into groups of special cells—muscle cells, nerve cells, blood cells, epithelial cells, connective tissue cells, and reproductive cells—exhibiting a division of labor in the performance of definite functions. Groups of cells organize into tissues, the tissues arrange themselves into patterns to form the various organs of the body, and the organs, in turn, group themselves into systems, such as the digestive, respiratory, nervous, skeletal, muscular, circulatory, urinary, and reproductive systems.

II—CELLS AND TISSUES OF THE BODY

A great deal has been learned about the cells and tissues which constitute the building materials of the body. But many basic problems remain to be solved. Investigators are constantly engaged in experiments to discover new facts about cells and tissues. A mere summary of scientific achievements in this field would require many volumes for presentation. Only a few of the most important findings can be included here.

CELLS

Cytology is the branch of anatomy dealing with cell structure and functions. The practical applications of this science to the diagnosis and treatment of disease have been numerous and significant. It is expected that continued research in cytology will enable man to control some of the worst of his ills. For example, recent studies of cell activity have advanced the knowledge about cancer and may eventually lead to effective measures against this disease.

Cell Structure

A cell consists of protoplasm and other substances, all enclosed within a membrane (a thin sheet of tissue). Cells range in size from .002 millimeters to 2 inches (ostrich egg). Figure 4 shows the two parts of a typical cell—the nucleus and the cytoplasm.

The cell nucleus includes the following: a membrane; particles called chromonemata (containing chromatin); tiny filaments (the linin net); and spherical bodies (nucleoli or karyosomes). The nucleus, located near the center of the cell, controls cell metabolism (cell growth and repair) and initiates reproduction of the cell. In cell division, the chromonemata are formed into chromosomes, which contain the hereditary particles, or *genes,* that influence the inheritance of traits from parents to offspring. Every human body cell has 46 chromosomes. (The human germ cell, i.e., sperm cell and egg cell or ovum, has 23 chromosomes;

6

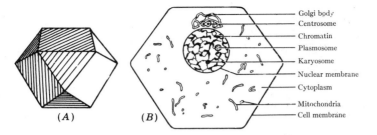

Golgi body
Centrosome
Chromatin
Plasmosome
Karyosome
Nuclear membrane
Cytoplasm
Mitochondria
Cell membrane

(A)   (B)

FIG. 4. Animal cell. A, surface view. B, cross section. (From Gordon Alexander, *Biology,* College Outline Series.)

consequently when two germ cells unite, each contributes **23** to the total of **46** chromosomes in the resulting body cell.)

The cytoplasm is the entire portion outside the nucleus. It includes the outer membrane of the cell, certain living components, and various lifeless parts. The living components (cell organoids) include smooth filaments or granules called mitochondria, the Golgi body of wavy threads or fibers, and the cell center with its centrosome surrounding the small, granular centrioles. The lifeless parts (cell inclusions) comprise fats, proteins, carbohydrates, crystals, and other temporary substances. The cytoplasm functions in cell secretion, absorption, conduction, and contraction.

Cell Functions

Cell activity depends upon the passage of food, oxygen, salts, and other materials through the outer membrane into the cytoplasm and the discharge of waste products to the outside. Cells vary in their ability to control the passage of specific substances. The degree of permeability is affected by the size of the openings in the membrane, the nature and size of the molecules of the substances attempting passage, and the electrical charge of the ions in the membrane as compared with the corresponding charge in the entering substances.

Particles may pass into the cell by means of diffusion, filtration, or osmosis. Diffusion is movement from a region of high to one of low concentration (as in the passage of oxygen from the lungs into the blood). Filtration is movement resulting from differences in mechanical pressure (as in the formation of urine in the kidneys). Osmosis is movement resulting from differences in the

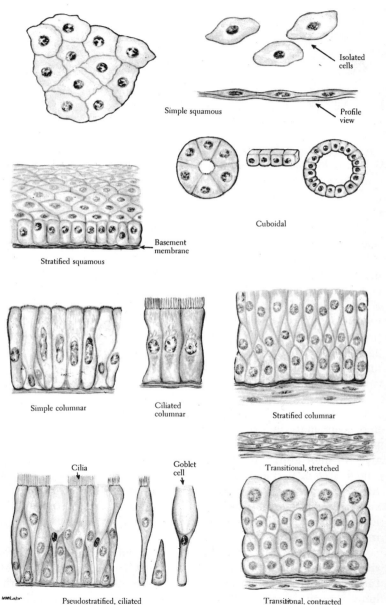

Isolated cells

Simple squamous

Profile view

Cuboidal

Basement membrane

Stratified squamous

Simple columnar

Ciliated columnar

Stratified columnar

Transitional, stretched

Cilia

Goblet cell

Pseudostratified, ciliated

Transitional, contracted

FIG. 5. Types of epithelial tissue.

pressures of dissolved substances on both sides of the cell membrane.

In addition to its basic activities as protoplasm (irritability, conductivity, contractility, metabolism, reproduction, and adaptation), each cell performs specialized functions depending on the type of cell. Thus, muscle cells specialize in contraction, nerve cells in the conduction of impulses, and epithelial cells in secretion. Some cells, for example certain nerve cells in brain centers, are necessary for life; others are of lesser importance. But all types of cells contribute something to the functions of the body as a whole.

TISSUES

Body tissues are of four kinds: epithelial tissue, connective tissue, muscle tissue, and nerve tissue. Epithelial tissue protects the body and produces secretions. Connective tissue joins and supports body structures. Muscle tissue contracts and relaxes, enabling organs and limbs to function. Nerve tissue activates and integrates the body and its parts. Specialized tissue derivatives include glands and membranes.

Epithelial Tissue

The surface of the body has a covering of epithelial tissue. This same type of tissue covers many internal organs, lines the blood vessels, the digestive and respiratory tracts, and the reproductive organs, and constitutes the secreting portions and ducts of glands. Epithelial tissue consists of cells packed closely together with intercellular fluid or cell cement. There may be only one layer of cells (simple epithelium), or there may be several layers (stratified epithelium).

Epithelial tissue may be squamous, cuboidal, columnar, or transitional. The squamous type has thin, flat cells and consists of single-layer cells lining the serous cavities (mesothelium), the cavities in connective tissue (mesenchymal epithelium), and the blood and lymph vessels (endothelium); it also includes stratified cells in the vagina, esophagus, cornea, and epidermis. The cuboidal type has cube-shaped cells, found in the smaller bronchi of the lungs, the gland ducts, and the kidney tubules. The columnar type has long, cylindrical cells, found in the pharynx, larynx, trachea, larger bronchi, intestines, and uterus.

The transitional type has several layers of large, rounded cells, found in the kidneys, ureter, and bladder, where tissues need to stretch and relax; these rounded cells are well suited to this requirement.

Connective Tissue

Connective tissue is composed primarily of intercellular material that is interspersed with relatively few cells. It is well supplied with blood or lymph; it is the most widely distributed of all tissue; its main functions are to bind muscles to bones, bones to bones, and tissues to each other, to form cartilage and bone, to store fat, to aid in the production of blood cells, and to provide immunity to disease.

There are two main classes of connective tissue, differing in their intercellular material: (1) connective tissue proper, with a fibrous material; (2) dense, connective tissue, with a semirigid or rigid material.

There are four types of connective tissue proper: (1) *mucous tissue,* of jelly-like (collagenous) material containing mucin and found only in the umbilical cord of the embryo; (2) *fibrous tissue* (including white fibrous, elastic, and areolar tissue), of semi-fluid material interlaced with white or yellow and white fibers, which forms the superficial fascia and interstitial tissue of most organs, surrounds blood vessels and nerves, and is found under epithelial layers of mucous and serous membranes; (3) *reticular tissue,* constituting the framework of lymph nodes, the spleen, and bone marrow and found in some endocrine glands and the digestive and respiratory passages; and (4) *adipose tissue,* consisting of cells equipped to store fat which protects organs from mechanical injury or excessive heat loss, holds organs in place, fills in angular areas of the body, and protects and supports the kidneys and eyes.

Dense connective tissues include cartilage and bone.

Cartilage is a tough, resilient substance which (except on the surfaces of joints) is covered by a fibrous membrane, the perichondrium. There are three types: (1) Hyaline cartilage consists of a uniform, rigid base (matrix) with collagenous fibers; its cells (chondrocytes), which lie in cavities (lacunae) are often single, but they may be grouped in twos or threes. Hyaline

CARTILAGE

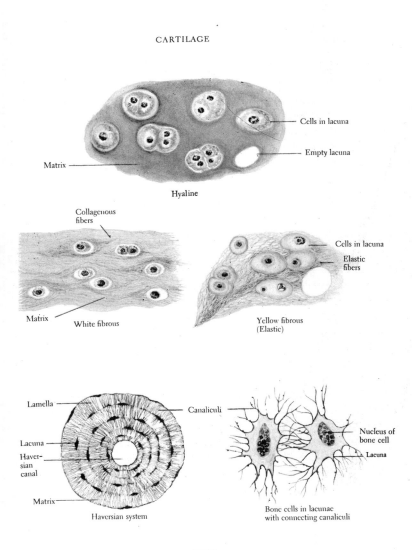

Cells in lacuna

Empty lacuna

Matrix

Hyaline

Collagenous fibers

Cells in lacuna

Elastic fibers

Matrix

White fibrous

Yellow fibrous
(Elastic)

Lamella

Canaliculi

Lacuna

Nucleus of
bone cell

Haver-
sian
canal

Lacuna

Matrix

Haversian system

Bone cells in lacunae
with connecting canaliculi

BONE

FIG. 6. Dense connective tissue.

cartilage is flexible and slightly elastic. It is found at the ends of bones and in the septum of the nose, as well as in the cartilage of the voice box and windpipe. (2) Fibrous cartilage consists of a less dense base with many collagenous fibers. It has greater strength and elasticity. It is found in the intervertebral discs between the vertebrae and in the symphysis pubis. (3) Elastic cartilage has many interlacing elastic fibers. It is more flexible and elastic than the other two types. It is found in the external ear, the Eustachian tube, and the voice box.

Bone is composed of an outer, hard layer and an inner, spongy core, resembling the structure of a reed. In the narrow outer layer, rigidity is provided by a compact matrix hardened by salts containing calcium and phosphorous. It is arranged in concentric layers, termed the Haversian system, which consists of a cylindrical matrix with a hollow center known as the Haversian canal. This canal carries blood vessels and nerves for the supply of the bone cells (osteocytes). The inner, spongy (cancellous) core harbors the yellow and red bone marrow. The yellow marrow stores fat cells; the red marrow contains red cells in varying stages of development.

The external surface of bones is covered by periosteum. This covering consists of an outer fibrous layer and an inner osteogenic (bone-forming) layer, which has the important function of feeding the underlying bone. Its cells (the osteoblasts) rebuild damaged bone. The covering membrane of cartilage (the perichondrium) has the function of nourishing the underlying cartilage. This function is particularly important because cartilage does not contain blood vessels. Bone is not an inert structure that remains unchanged after attaining full growth. On the contrary, it is a living tissue which undergoes constant structural change in response to changes of mechanical stress and to variations in the mineral contents of the body. These changes are under the control of the parathyroid glands which stimulate the osteoclasts (large cells with multiple nuclei) to remove bone and stimulate the osteoblasts to build up bone as needed. This system of control explains how bones can be molded and grow stronger or lighter in response to varying demands.

If all the mineral content of a bone is dissolved, the organic matrix will remain. It is a firm structure, and it retains the shape of the original bone.

Muscle and Nerve Tissues

Two specialized types of body tissue are muscular tissue and nervous tissue.

The cells of muscular tissue contract and relax, thus creating mechanical energy required for movement of the body and its parts. Muscle cells are arranged in groups as fibers, embedded in connective tissue to which they are bound by intercellular substance. There are three kinds of muscular tissue: smooth, striated, and cardiac. *Smooth muscle tissue* consists of long cells in sheets, layers, or bundles, and the cytoplasm of each cell contains the contractile elements, or myofibrils; it is found in the wall of the digestive tract, walls of blood vessels, the urinary bladder and gallbladder, the genital ducts, the bronchi and trachea, and the iris; its action is involuntary. *Striated muscle tissue* consists of bundles of fibers made up of large nucleated cells with myofibrils that have alternating dark and light bands, giving the fibers a striped appearance; it is found in skeletal muscles, muscles of the tongue and soft palate, the scalp, the pharynx, the upper esophagus, and the eye; in most cases, its action is voluntary. *Cardiac muscle tissue*, the heart muscle, consists of a network of branching fibers connected to adjoining fibers, having striated cells and transverse markings called intercalated discs; its action is involuntary, automatic, and rhythmic. Within the heart, too, are special muscle fibers, the Purkinje fibers, which have fainter striations, fewer myofibrils, and more intercellular material than the typical heart muscle; they constitute the impulse-conducting system of the heart.

Nerve tissue consists of two kinds of cells: (1) nerve cells (neurons) and (2) connecting or supporting cells (neuroglia). Nerve tissue is found in the brain, in the spinal cord, and in nerves throughout the body. The cells of nerve tissue function in the reception of stimuli, the conduction of nerve impulses, and the excitation of responses to stimuli. The function of receiving and transmitting nerve impulses makes possible the coordination and integration of all bodily activities. (For a description of nerve cells and the chief structures of the nervous system, see page 43.)

Epithelial cells grow into adjacent underlying connective tissue to form glands. These are masses of cells which obtain materials from the blood or lymph (a principal body fluid) and transform them for absorption by or discharge from the body. There are two kinds of glands, namely, the duct—or exocrine—and the ductless—or endocrine—glands. Duct glands (e.g., salivary glands or sweat glands) remain attached to the epithelial tissue and empty their secretions onto a surface. Ductless glands (e.g., the thyroid) separate from epithelial tissue and discharge secretions into blood or lymph. (The pancreas and the liver combine exocrine and endocrine functions, discharging one type of secretions through ducts, other types directly into the blood.)

Glands differ in their secretions. They may secrete serous fluids, or mucous fluids, or both (mixed glands). They may be simple, without branches, or compound, with two or more branches. They may remain tube-shaped throughout their growth (tubular glands), or they may end in enlarged secretory portions (alveolar glands). Tubular glands include the sweat glands, gastric glands and glands in the large intestine, kidneys, and liver. Alveolar glands include the sebaceous glands and the mammary glands. Finally, there is a compound tubulo-alveolar type, such as the pancreas and the salivary glands.

Membranes

Membranes are tissues arranged as sheets which function as covering or connecting structures. They consist of epithelium and connective tissue. The skin (cutaneous membrane) is a protective covering. *Mucous membranes* line all passages leading from the surface of the body to internal structures, as in the digestive, respiratory, urinary, and reproductive systems. *Serous membranes* line the walls of body cavities (as well as the surfaces of organs located within these cavities) to provide lubrication of moving parts; examples of these membranes are (1) the pleura around the lungs, (2) the peritoneum in the abdomen, and (3) the conjunctiva inside the eyeballs and over the exposed parts of the eyeball. The *synovial membranes* line the interior of joints and of bursae. Membranes lining the heart and blood vessels are called *endothelium*. Note that some membranes perform specialized functions; e.g., the ear drum closing the ear canal transmits sound vibrations to the inner ear. Epithelial covering cells vary in structure according to local requirements; thus, the skin is covered by layers of stratified squamous epithelium, whereas mucous membranes are lined by columnar secreting cells.

III—THE SKIN

Dermatology is the branch of anatomy that deals with the skin (*integument*) and its derivatives, including the sweat glands, oil glands, mammary glands, hair, and nails.

The main functions of the skin are to keep out foreign substances (including some infectious organisms) and protect the underlying tissues from injury, maintain adequate moisture in the tissues, regulate body heat and temperature, act as the receptor organ for the senses of touch and pain, and aid in the elimination of water and waste materials.

STRUCTURE OF THE SKIN

The illustrations on page 144 show the two main portions of the skin: the superficial *epidermis* and the deep *dermis* or *corium*. The epidermis, which has no blood vessels, consists of four layers of cells—in order of their distance from the surface, the stratum corneum, stratum lucidum, stratum granulosum, and stratum germinativum. The cells of the deepest layer (the stratum germinativum) multiply rapidly, rising into the top layer of the skin where, since there are no blood vessels, they are deprived of nourishment, die, and are continuously being shed. (These cells sometimes contain an abundance of melanin, a pigment in the form of dark granules that gives the skin a brown or black coloring.) The dermis, or *true skin*, consists of elastic, fibrous connective tissue generally much thicker than the epidermis (though very thin in the eyelids and scrotum) and contains numerous blood and lymph vessels, nerves, smooth muscle fibers, glands, hair follicles, and fat deposits. It has an upper papillary layer, from which projections reach into the epidermis, and a lower reticular layer composed of interlacing bundles of white fibers and elastic tissue that imparts elasticity to the skin.

GLANDS

Sebaceous or *oil glands* and *sudoriferous* or *sweat glands* are among the accessory organs of the skin. Sebaceous glands,

15

secreting oil from disintegrating cells, empty either into hair
follicles or directly onto the skin surface.   Many are found on
the nose and cheeks, where disorders such as blackheads often
develop if the oily secretion (*sebum*) is excessive instead of being
freely discharged.   Sudoriferous glands, tube-shaped, are found
in the skin surface of most parts of the body, especially the
forehead, palms and soles, and axillary regions.   The average
daily excretion of sweat totals about one pint.   Nerve centers
in the brain and spine regulate the action of these glands, which
increases markedly in fright, nervousness, or severe pain.   (Modified sudoriferous glands are the *ceruminous glands* of the inner
ear, which secrete wax; *ciliary glands* at the edges of the eyelids; and *Montgomery's glands* on the skin around the nipple.)

Specialized for the production of milk are the two *mammary
glands*, extending from the second to the sixth rib.   Each has
cone-shaped tissue (corpus mammae) with branching lobes,
lobules, a projecting, pigmented nipple, arteries, veins, nerves,
and lymph pathways connecting with nearby and distant lymph
nodes.   Cancer cells often spread from one breast to the other
or to distant organs along these lymph pathways.

HAIR

The special functions of hair include the retention of body
heat and the magnification of the sense of touch.   The removal
of hair from hairy spots in the skin is known to reduce their
sensitivity to touch.

The parts of a single hair include the *shaft*, extending upward
from a pit in or near the surface of the epidermis; the *root*, embedded in the corium and surrounded by an epidermal down-
growth, the *hair follicle;* and the *hair bulb*, the expanded base of
the root into which, from underneath, a dermal papilla (connective tissue) of nerves and capillaries projects.   (See illustration of hairy skin, page 144.)   A single hair has three layers of
cells: the external layer, or cuticle; the horny portion, or cortex
(actually consisting of several layers) ; and the central row of
cells, the medulla (not present in some hairs).   Hair cells contain
a pigment responsible for variations in hair coloring; if the
pigmentation is inadequate, the air between the cells reflects light
that makes the hair appear silvery or gray.

In the bulb of the hair root are the live, germinating cells which multiply and cause the shafts (dead cells) to rise upward to be replaced by younger cells. Scalp hairs grow at the rate of about five inches per year during their life period of two to five years; eyebrows and eyelashes can grow for several months at most, before replacement. Sex hormones have a pronounced effect on the extent and location of hair growth, as seen in the faces of males and in the pubic and axillary regions of males and females.

The hair follicle, surrounding the root, has an inner, epithelial sheath and an outer, connective tissue sheath. The inner sheath consists of three layers of cells (the horny cuticle, Huxley's layers of flat cells, and Henle's layer of tube-shaped cells) and an outer layer merging with the deep stratum germinativum of the epidermis. The outer, connective tissue sheath, growing out of the corium, surrounds the inner sheath. A specialized muscle, the *arrector pili muscle*, attached to the connective tissue sheath, contracts in times of stress so that the hair stands on end ("goose flesh"). The same muscle presses the sebaceous glands, aiding in the discharge of their oil secretion.

NAILS

On the dorsal surfaces of the digits and toes are the nails, horny plates consisting of the following parts: a visible portion attached to the digit or toe, which it protects; a free edge in the distal portion; and a root, the covered portion embedded in the skin. The nail bed is the skin under the nail; the nail wall is the skin covering the root and sides of the nail. The lunula is the white portion at the base of the nail. Since the body of the nail is somewhat transparent, the blood shows through and gives it a pinkish hue. Cells in the stratum germinativum near the nail root fuse with the root cells and push the older cells away so that the nail grows; the rate of growth is about a tenth of a millimeter daily for fingernails and about half that rate for toenails. If the surrounding area (the stratum germinativum or matrix) is intact, a nail that has been torn off will regenerate.

PRACTICAL CONSIDERATIONS

The temperature of the body is controlled by the involuntary (autonomic) nervous system through changes in the volume of blood flowing through the skin. An increase in the diameter (dilation) of the smallest blood vessels (arterioles and capillaries) causes a loss of heat and a reddening of the skin (flushes). A similar mechanism causes blushing of face or chest. Excessive redness is also present in generalized (systemic) disorders of the body, such as high blood pressure, and in fever. The reverse condition, pallor, may be caused by a narrowing of the skin arteries—often as a means of preserving body heat in a cold environment. Skin pallor is also noted in anemia, shock, and fright. A bluish tinge (cyanosis), especially of the lips, may be an indication of an inadequate supply of oxygen, as in certain abnormalities (or failure) of the heart. A yellow tinge of the skin is found in jaundice. It is produced by the entry of bile into the blood stream as a consequence of liver disorder.

It has been discovered that sunlight and ultraviolet radiation are absorbed through the skin, where they cause chemical changes activating the sex hormones and aiding in the production of vitamin D (preventing rickets). An excess of such radiation may cause serious burns, as well as skin growths, including cancer.

Among the most common afflictions of the skin are those resulting from mechanical injury (trauma), such as cuts and abrasions. Local infections include the familiar boils, abscesses, and acne. Generalized disorders of the body may also cause various skin manifestations; examples of such disorders are allergies (as in hives), shingles, and infectious fevers (as in measles and in scarlet fever). There are also a large number of specific skin diseases, such as psoriasis (indicated by red patches of skin covered with white scales) and seborrhea (involving the excessive discharge of secretions onto the skin).

Recent experiments by Professors Vojin Popovic and Roberto Masironi, of the Department of Physiology at Emory University, appear to have demonstrated the validity of the *differential hypothermia* hypothesis to explain the disappearance of transplanted cancers in golden hamsters. This hypothesis is based on the differences in the metabolic rates and energy requirements of normal and rapidly growing types of transplanted malignant cells. In several hundreds of cases treated, cancers which were kept warm while the rest of the body was cooled were eradicated and did not recur. Dr. Popovic's experiments also verified the assumption that the effects of anticancer drugs on transplanted cancers would be enhanced by differential hypothermia.

IV—THE SKELETAL SYSTEM

Osteology (from the Greek *osteon*, meaning *bone*) is the branch of anatomy that describes the structure and functions of the skeletal system. The adult skeleton is composed of some 206 bones, numerous ligaments, and cartilage.

FUNCTIONS OF BONES, LIGAMENTS, AND CARTILAGE

Bones provide a firm framework that gives shape to the body and supports its parts. They protect vital organs, such as the heart, brain, and lungs, from injury. They facilitate bodily movements by acting in cooperation with numerous muscles attached to the bones by tendons. They store reserves of calcium, nearly all of the body's calcium being stored in the skeleton. They manufacture blood cells (a function performed by red bone marrow).

The main function of ligaments is to hold the bones together in the joints, or articulations—where ligaments (consisting of dense, fibrous tissue) or other types of body tissues connect the extremities of bones.

Cartilage furnishes elastic, supporting connective tissues which protect the bones at the joints from shock and give the skeleton more flexibility.

In the embryo, most of the skeleton consists of cartilage. The temporary cartilage model is gradually absorbed and replaced by permanent bone through the invasion of blood vessels and osteoblasts (bone-forming cells) from the perichondrium, which gradually assumes the structure of the periosteum. In the long bones of the limbs, the ends (epiphyses) remain cartilaginous for years. Centers of ossification (bone formation) appear, first, in the middle of the bones and, subsequently, in the epiphyses. Even after complete ossification of the epiphyses, a narrow layer of cartilage remains between the epiphysis and the shaft (diaphysis) of the bone. Growth in length continues at this epiphyseal line, while growth in thickness is achieved through the deposition of new bone by the osteoblasts lining the periosteum.

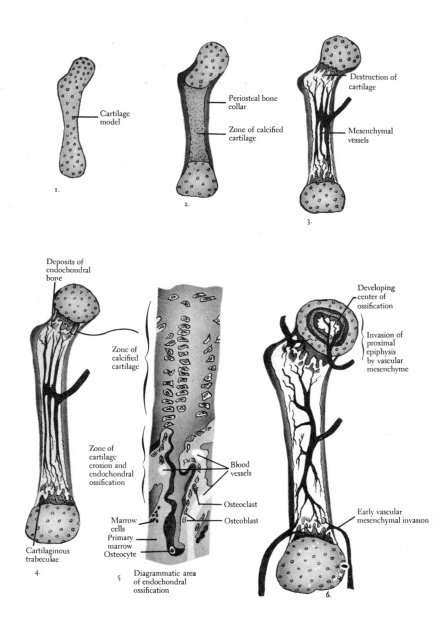

FIG. 7. Early stages in the growth of a long bone.

Final bony fusion of all separate parts of the bone marks the end of the period of growth. This process occurs at varying ages in different bones, generally during the period from puberty to the twenty-fifth year.

The endocrine glands exert important controls over the growth of bone. Thus, the "growth hormone" from the anterior lobe of the pituitary gland stimulates bone growth in length, whereas hormones from the gonads (testes and ovaries) bring about cessation of growth by causing fusion of the shaft of the bone with its epiphyses.

STRUCTURE OF BONES

As already stated, all bones consist of an outer, dense material (compact bone) and an inner, spongy, more porous material (cancellous bone). But the relative amounts of these two types of material vary with the specific bones, as well as with the different portions of a single bone. There are four main classes of bones: long, short, flat, and irregular. The long bones, present only in the extremities, are cylindrical and consist of the following parts: the shaft or body (diaphysis); the end portions (epiphyses); the fibrous membrane (periosteum) covering the outer bone surface around the shaft; the medullary cavity extending within the shaft and containing yellow bone marrow; and the membrane (endosteum) lining the medullary cavity. The short bones, such as those of the wrist and ankle, consist of a heavy shaft of spongy, elastic material within a thin outside layer of compact bone. The flat bones, such as the ribs and sternum (breast bone), consist of spongy material between two platelike coverings of compact bone, thus protecting internal organs and providing flat surfaces for the attachment of muscles. The irregular bones, including the vertebrae, are rather like the short bones in makeup and contain red bone marrow of great significance in the formation of blood cells.

BONES OF THE SKELETON

The skeletal system consists of two divisions: the axial skeleton and the appendicular skeleton. The axial skeleton, the main framework of the body, consists of the bones of the spine, skull, and chest. The appendicular skeleton consists of the bones of the upper and lower extremities. An infant may have about 350 bones, many of which fuse during the process of growth. Adults vary somewhat in the number of bones, but a total of 206 bones, shown in the accompanying table, is considered normal or typical.

Axial Skeleton (80 Bones)

Spine (26 Bones)

 Cervical bones—upper 7 vertebrae (7)
 Thoracic bones—next 12 vertebrae (12)
 Lumbar bones—next 5 vertebrae, supporting small of back (5)
 Sacrum—lower end of spine (1)
 Coccyx—vestige of tail (1)

Skull (29 Bones)

 Bones of cranium (8):
  Frontal—forehead (1)
  Occipital—posterior floor and back of cranium (1)
  Sphenoid—across midportion of floor and sides of cranium (1)
  Ethmoid—front of cranium floor and medial walls of orbit (1)
  Parietal—side walls of cranium behind the frontal (2)
  Temporal—lower sides of cranium and part of floor (2)
 Bones of face (14):
  Mandible—lower jaw (1)
  Vomer—lower part of nasal septum (1)
  Maxilla—upper jaw (2)
  Zygomatic—cheek bones (2)
  Lacrimal—front part of medial wall of orbit (2)

 Nasal—superior part of bridge of nose (2)

  Inferior nasal conchae—inner surface of nasal side wall (2)
  Palatine—posterior of hard palate, nasal floor and side (2)

 Hyoid bone—in throat, between mandible and upper larynx (1)
 Ear ossicles—middle-ear bones, within temporal bone (6)

Chest (25 Bones)

 Sternum—breast bone (1)
 Ribs (24)

  True ribs—upper 7 pairs, attached to sternum (14)
  False ribs—5 pairs, including 2 pairs of floating ribs (10)

Appendicular Skeleton (126 Bones)

Upper Extremities (64 Bones)
 Clavicles—collar bones (2)
 Scapula—shoulder blade (2)
 Humerus—upper arms (2)
 Radius—thumb side of forearm (2)
 Ulna—other side of forearm (2)
 Carpals—2 rows, end of hand; wrist bones (16)
 Metacarpals—palm of hand (10)
 Phalanges—fingers, thumb (28)
Lower Extremities (62 Bones)
 Pelvic bones—hip (2)

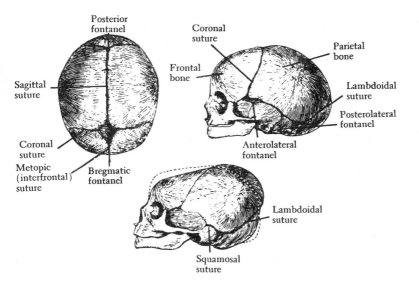

FIG. 8. Three views of skull of new-born infant, showing sutures and fontanels. In the lower drawing, the molded head is shown: the dotted lines indicate the alteration that takes place during birth.

Lower Extremities (62 Bones—Cont.)
   Femur—thigh (2)
   Patella—kneecap (2)
   Tibia—shin (2)
   Fibula—side of lower leg (2)
   Tarsals—instep (14)
   Metatarsals—feet (10)
   Phalanges—toes (28)

There are a variable number of sesamoid bones (only the largest of which, the patella, is listed in the table) so called because they resemble sesame seeds; they are found in the thumb and large toe and elsewhere in tendons subject to considerable pressure. Other small bones, the wormian bones, are sometimes found in the joints (called *sutures*) of the cranial bones, but most of these joints fuse in the adult. In the infant at birth are soft areas, membrane-covered spaces between cranial bones, allowing some skull compression during delivery; these soft areas, called *fontanels*, disappear as the membranes turn into bone.

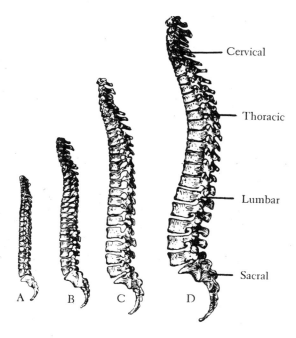

Cervical

Thoracic

Lumbar

Sacral

A   B   C   D

FIG. 9. Vertebral column of (A) new-born child; (B) three-year-old child; (C) ten-year-old child; (D) adult.

The Spine

The spine is a vertical column (the backbone) consisting of a series of 26 connected bony segments (vertebrae), extending in a curved line (with four curves) from the head to the coccyx (vestige of a tail). Being segmented, it is flexible rather than rigid. In accordance with the need for carrying increased weight, the lower vertebrae are larger than the upper ones; the four curves also increase the carrying strength of the column. The illustration shows the stages of development of the spine from birth to adulthood. It should be noted that the thoracic and sacral curves are present at birth, whereas the cervical and lumbar curves develop after birth.

In a front view of the skeleton, the spine is seen as the central axis, to which are attached the skull, ribs, and pelvic girdle (a bony ring comprising two hip bones, the sacrum, and the coccyx) ;

and enclosed within the vertebral column are the protected spinal cord and the roots of spinal nerves. The 26 vertebrae of the spine differ markedly in size but are similar in structure. All except the first cervical vertebra have a body—a solid, flat, oval portion connected to the bodies of adjacent vertebrae by means of fibrous, cartilaginous discs and various ligaments. All have a posterior portion—the vertebral arch with its opening (the vertebral foramen) for the spinal cord. The arch has two projections (pedicles) from the posterior of the body; two laminae, or flat plates of bone as continuations of the pedicles; and seven extensions (processes) that project from the laminae. A notch on the posterior surface of each pedicle provides an opening for the spinal nerves extending from the cord.

During the process of growth, the exceptional first cervical vertebra (the *atlas*) loses part of what would normally become its body to the second cervical vertebra (the *axis*); this gives the latter an extension upward of its body (the extension being called the *dens*), providing a pivot for rotation of the atlas in movements of the head. The cervical vertebrae provide the framework of the neck.

The Chest

The thorax (or bony cage of the chest) consists of 12 thoracic vertebrae, the 12 ribs, and the sternum (breast bone). All 12 pairs of ribs have posterior connections with the vertebrae, but some do not have direct anterior connections. The upper 7 ribs, terminating in cartilage, completely enclose the thorax as they join the sternum directly, but the 8th, 9th, and 10th ribs (also with cartilage ends) attach to the cartilage of the rib above each of them, thus forming a cartilaginous margin to the lower boundary of the thorax in front. The 11th and 12th ribs remain unattached to bone at their forward ends, although they are embedded in muscle and other soft parts. From the 1st to the 7th the ribs increase in length; from the 8th on, they become shorter. A typical rib is a thin, curved strip of bone with a head (an expanded posterior part where, at two flat surfaces, or facets, the rib connects with the bodies of two adjacent vertebrae); a neck, about 2.5 cm. long—extending from the head and with a crest for the attachment of a ligament; a tubercle—a somewhat raised portion at the junction of shaft and neck, with a facet for connecting the rib to an extension of a vertebra; a

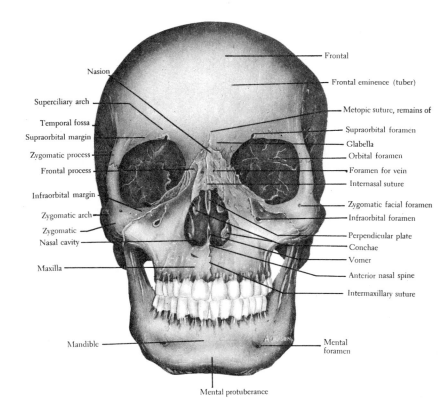

Nasion

Superciliary arch

Temporal fossa

Supraorbital margin

Zygomatic process

Frontal process

Infraorbital margin

Zygomatic arch

Zygomatic

Nasal cavity

Maxilla

Mandible

Mental protuberance

Frontal

Frontal eminence (tuber)

Metopic suture, remains of

Supraorbital foramen

Glabella

Orbital foramen

Foramen for vein

Internasal suture

Zygomatic facial foramen

Infraorbital foramen

Perpendicular plate

Conchae

Vomer

Anterior nasal spine

Intermaxillary suture

Mental foramen

Fɪɢ. 10. Anterior view of skull.

shaft—the thin, flat, markedly curved body of the rib; an angle where the shaft curves abruptly; and a costal groove along the inferior border of the shaft, providing a channel for blood vessels and nerves. The end of the shaft near the sternum has a cupped shape fitted to the connecting costal cartilage. (Exceptions to this typical structure of a rib are found in the 1st rib, which has no angle or groove; in the 2nd rib, which has a pronounced eminence on its posterior surface; and in the 11th and 12th, the floating ribs, which have no angle, groove, tubercle, or neck.)

The Skull

The 29 bones of the skull include those of the cranium and face, the hyoid bone, and the ear ossicles. The 8 cranial bones enclose a cavity within which are the brain, 3 layers of protective membranes (dura mater, arachnoid, and pia mater), and numerous blood vessels. Fourteen irregular bones, including the lower and upper jaw bones, nasal bones, and cheek bones, form the bony framework of the face.

The human skull, compared with the skulls of other animals, displays a relative decrease in the size of the face and a relative increase in the size of the cranium. There are actually 5 great cavities of the skull: two cavities, or orbits, enclosing the eyes; the nasal cavity, with its two chambers separated by the septum; the oral cavity, with the jaw bones and maxillae, palatine, and sphenoid bones; and the cranial cavity.

There are important cavities, called paranasal sinuses, in the walls of some of the skull bones adjacent to the nasal cavity. These sinuses have a lining of ciliated mucous membrane which is continuous with that of the nasal cavity, and they drain into the nasal passageways and help to moisten them. The paranasal sinuses are useful resonating chambers for the voice. The continuity of the membrane with that of the nose and mouth permits infectious material to spread rapidly through the various passageways, as in the common cold.

The U-shaped bone in the neck, the hyoid bone, is the only bone that does not meet with other bones to form a joint; ligaments connect it with an extension of the temporal bone. Some of the muscles of the tongue and mouth insert in the hyoid.

The Upper Extremities

The shoulder girdle consists of two scapulae (shoulder blades) and two clavicles (collar bones). The scapula is a flat bone of triangular shape attached by means of muscles to the back of the thorax and constituting the prominence of the shoulder. Its convex posterior surface has a ridge, the spine, and ends laterally in a projection, the acromion. Here it is attached to the elongate clavicle, which serves as a prop for the shoulder and, in turn, connects with the sternum, creating a sturdy girdle with considerable movability.

The humerus is the long bone of the upper arm. It consists of a shaft and two large extremities. It is attached at one large end to the glenoid cavity of the scapula, at the other to the two bones of the forearm—the radius and the ulna. At the head end are two rounded processes (the greater and lesser tubercles) enclosing a deep groove (the intertubercular groove) for the tendon of the biceps muscle. On the posterior side of the shaft is a groove for passage of an important nerve, the radial nerve; midway down the side of the shaft is a rough area (the deltoid tuberosity), into which the deltoid muscle inserts. At the other large end, a rounded knob (the capitulum) connects with the radius; a projection (the trochlea) connects with the ulna; a depression (the olecranon fossa) accommodates an extension of the ulna when the lower arm is extended; and another depression (the coronoid fossa) connects similarly with the ulna when the arm is flexed.

The ulna and the radius are the two bones of the forearm, the radius being lateral to the ulna. The end of the ulna nearest to the upper arm connects with the humerus and radius, aiding in motion that turns the hand so that the palm can face forward or backward. The ulna extends beyond the radius, having an olecranon process (the elbow) next to the humerus, with a notch connecting it to the trochlea of the humerus. The other end has a small, round process, the head, with a connecting surface for the radius; it also articulates with the wrist bones by means of a disc of fibrocartilage. The radius has a head connecting with the radial head of the humerus and with the radial notch of the ulna; a projection (radial tuberosity) into which the biceps muscle inserts; and a protrusion on the opposite end called the styloid process. Below the forearm is the wrist

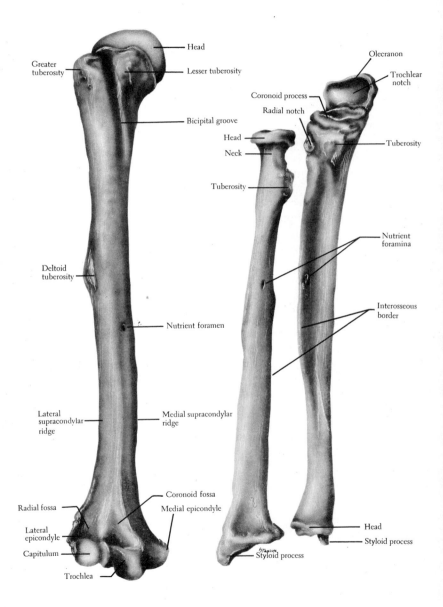

FIG. 11. Humerus, radius, and ulna.

composed of 8 small bones, then the body of the hand with
its skeleton of 5 bones, to which the 12 bones of the fingers and
2 bones of the thumb are attached in series.

The Lower Extremities

On each side of the sacrum are two broad, curved bones that
meet in front. The large space between these three bones is the
pelvic cavity. Together with the sacrum and coccyx, they form
the pelvic girdle—serving as a base for the attachment of the
bones of the lower extremities and as a protective frame for the
organs of the urinary and reproductive systems. Each hip bone
(*os coxae*, or *os innominatum*) is a fusion of three separate bones
—the ilium, the ischium, and the pubis. (The ilium is the largest,
fan-shaped, and uppermost; the ischium is the V-shaped bottom
portion, heavy and strong because of the weight it must bear; the
pubis is a curved bone forming the anterior and inferior portion.)
The three parts extend toward the center of the hip bone to
form a deep cavity (the acetabulum) into which the head of
the thigh bone (femur) fits. (See chart, page 118.)

The femur is the strongest and longest bone of the body, com-

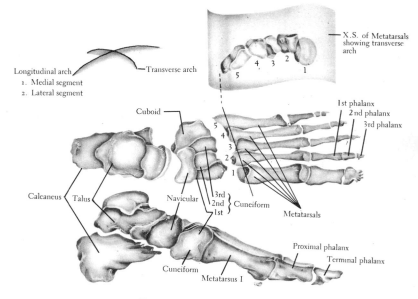

FIG. 12. Bones of the foot.

parable to the humerus of the arm in the upper extremities. The
tibia and fibula of the leg are similar to the radius and ulna of the
arm. The patella (kneecap), the largest sesamoid bone, is in the
tendon of the quadriceps femoris muscle that moves the lower leg.
The tarsal bones of the foot—comparable to the bones of the wrist
but totalling 7 instead of 8 in number—form the heel and
back portion of the foot; here the tendons, blood vessels, and
nerves must turn forward in line with the shift from the vertical
bones of the leg to the horizontal bones of the foot. The 5 long
bones (metatarsals) of the foot and the 14 bones (phalanges) of
the toes correspond to the metacarpals of the hand and the
phalanges of the fingers and thumb, respectively.

JOINTS

Joints are the junctions (meeting places called articulations)
between bones or between cartilage and bone. There are two
main kinds of joints: (1) those (called synarthroses) with little
or no movement and without a cavity; and (2) those (called
diarthroses) with varying degrees of free movement and with a
cavity between their surfaces that contains a lubricating fluid
(synovial fluid).

Examples of the synarthroses are the joints between the tibia
and fibula, with slight movement (syndesmosis, bound by ligaments of fibrous connective tissue); those at the junction of the
two hip bones (the pubic symphysis), with slight movement
(synchondrosis, bound by hyaline cartilage); and those between
cranial bones, with no movement at all (synostosis, bound by
fibrous cartilage). Examples of the diarthroses are the joints
of the limbs, with gliding movements between carpal bones, hinge
movements between the humerus and ulna, ball-and-socket movements of the hip, pivot movements of the radius and ulna, ellip-
soidal movements between the carpals and the radius, and saddle
movements between the carpal bone and the 1st metacarpal bone
of the thumb.

The direction of these joint movements (at freely moving
diarthrodial joints) is indicated by means of special terms, as
follows: *flexion* (movement that reduces the angle between the
bones, as in bending the arm at the elbow); *extension* (movement
that increases the angle between bones and is thus opposite to
flexion); *abduction* (movement away from the midline of the

body, as in sidewise movement of the leg); *adduction* (movement toward the midline of the body, the opposite of abduction); *supination* (clockwise movement of the hand, turning the palm forward); *pronation* (counterclockwise movement of the hand, turning the palm backward); *circumduction* (circular movement, as in a circular swinging of the arm); *inversion* (ankle movement that turns the foot inward); *eversion* (ankle movement that turns the foot outward); *elevation* (movement that raises the bone, muscle, or limb); *depression* (opposite of elevation); *protraction* (forward movement); *retraction* (backward movement); *hyperextension* (movement that bends the part beyond the position taken in extension); *plantar flexion* (movement that flexes the foot toward the sole); and *dorsiflexion* (plantar extension with upward movement of the foot).

The typical freely moving joint has (in addition to the cartilage that covers the surface) a two-layered capsule within which the joint is enclosed; the joint cavity, containing the synovial lubricating fluid; and the ligaments consisting of fibers of connective tissue. The ligaments connect the bones to each other and to some extent control their movement. There may also be a disc of cartilage dividing the joint into two parts, as in the joint of the jaw bone and temporal bone.

DISORDERS OF THE SKELETAL SYSTEM

Since it is the function of bones to supply rigidity to the body, they bear the brunt of external violence and are, therefore, subject to injuries (trauma), such as dislocations, cracks, and fractures.

In dislocations, the ends of the bones forming the affected joint are forced out of alignment with varying degrees of tearing of tendons, ligaments, and the joint capsule. Herniation of an intervertebral disc is a notable example of dislocation. The protrusion of the disc results in pressure against nerve structures which causes pain and disability.

A simple fracture is one that occurs without a break in the overlying skin; a compound fracture is one in which the tissue is broken and the bones are exposed. The compound type is much more serious because the bones may become infected. If the broken ends of a bone cannot be aligned by means of external manipulation, it may become necessary to "reduce" the separated fragments by open operation. A metal pin may have to be inserted to ensure healing in the correct position.

Fractures of the skull and vertebral column are particularly serious because of possible damage to the brain or spinal cord. For this reason the victim of such an injury must not be moved until expert care can be given.

Joints are subject to various afflictions, such as the following: (1) infections (as in tuberculosis and gonorrhea) which may in some cases cause ankylosis (a complete fusion of the adjoining bones, with loss of mobility):

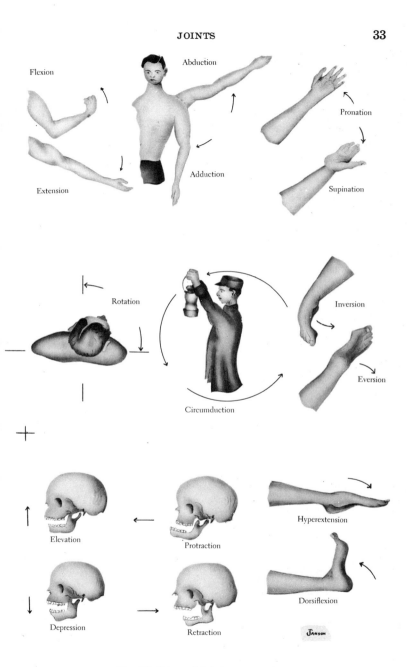

FIG. 13. Types of joint movements.

(2) rheumatic fever; (3) rheumatoid arthritis (with ultimate erosion of cartilage, enlargement of the bones around the joint, and ankylosis); and (4) osteoarthritis (with destruction of cartilage and bone). In gout, a disturbance of metabolism with an excess of uric acid in the blood, extremely painful swellings of joints characterize the acute phase. In growing children, lack of vitamin D and of sunlight interferes with the utilization of calcium and phosphorus and may cause rickets (characterized by softening of the bones and by deformities such as knock-knee and bowlegs).

Bursitis is a painful swelling, occasionally with calcium deposition, of a bursa (a sac-like pouch filled with lubricating fluid). Bursae are situated around joints and tendons, where they provide protection against pressure or friction. "Housemaid's knee" is a term applied to inflammation of the bursa covering the kneecap.

V—THE MUSCULAR SYSTEM

Myology is the branch of anatomy that describes the muscular system—its tissue components, structure, and functions. The discussion ,of the body tissues described three types of muscle tissue: smooth, cardiac, and striated. The first two types are involuntary, the third voluntary (normally subject to conscious control). Smooth muscles, in the walls of the intestine and the blood vessels, and cardiac muscle are stimulated by impulses from fibers of the autonomic nervous system; if the external nerves are cut, these muscles, nevertheless, continue to function. Striated muscles, in the skeletal system, are stimulated by impulses from fibers of cerebrospinal nerves; if the nerves are cut, the muscles are paralyzed.

There is not always a clear separation between voluntary and involuntary functions, inasmuch as on occasion some typically voluntary functions may occur involuntarily. Conversely, certain ordinarily involuntary actions may sometimes be controllable by conscious effort. Nevertheless, the distinction is generally applicable.

SMOOTH MUSCLES

Smooth muscle tissue is present in the walls of the digestive tract, the walls of blood vessels, the gallbladder and urinary passages and bladder, the genital ducts and the womb, the trachea and bronchi, the spleen, and the eye. Smooth muscles perform four kinds of involuntary action: they propel materials through passageways of the body (e.g., food along the intestinal tract) ; they expel materials from the body (e.g., bile from the gallbladder) ; they constrict or dilate openings (e.g., the pupil of the eye) ; and they contract or expand the width of tubes (e.g., arteries and veins).

CARDIAC MUSCLE

Cardiac muscle tissue constitutes the wall of the heart. The heart muscle is a good illustration of the effect of work upon

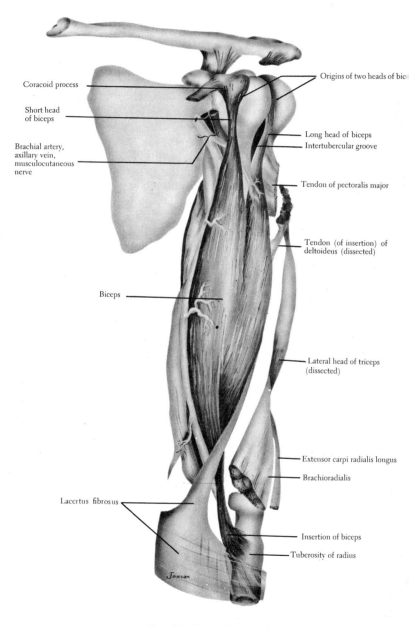

Coracoid process

Short head
of biceps

Brachial artery,
axillary vein,
musculocutaneous
nerve

Biceps

Lacertus fibrosus

Origins of two heads of bic

Long head of biceps
Intertubercular groove

Tendon of pectoralis major

Tendon (of insertion) of
deltoideus (dissected)

Lateral head of triceps
(dissected)

Extensor carpi radialis longus

Brachioradialis

Insertion of biceps
Tuberosity of radius

Fig. 14. An entire muscle.

the size and strength of a muscle. Note in the upper figure on page 127 that the tissue in the upper chamber, the atrium, is much thinner than the tissue in the lower chamber, the ventricle. This is because the ventricle pumps blood to a greater distance, performing more work and therefore requiring more muscular power.

SKELETAL MUSCLE

The voluntary actions of skeletal muscles involve the control of body posture and a wide variety of movements of body parts. Movements include locomotion and other activity of limbs, manipulation by fingers, vocalization by tongue and lips, swallowing, motion of the eyes, and activity of the abdominal muscles to assist respiration and defecation.

Contraction

When an effective stimulus, such as a nerve impulse (produced by an internal or external force—e.g., electrical, chemical, or thermal) affects a skeletal muscle, one or more fibers contract; as the strength of the stimulus increases, more fibers are activated. In the case of the heart muscle, however, any stimulus strong enough to be at all effective causes the entire muscle to contract. Continuous contraction gradually deprives muscles temporarily of their ability to contract, the condition being characterized as muscular fatigue. (In the infectious disease lockjaw or tetanus, caused by the bacterium *Clostridium tetani*, certain voluntary muscles remain locked in contraction, unable to relax. Similarly in severe malocclusion of the teeth, muscle spasms may lock the mouth open or tightly closed if the head of the mandible, the condyle, slips out of its socket.) Normally, however, healthy muscles can relax and recover from the effects of repeated, continuous contractions.

Leverage

Skeletal muscles work on the principle of a lever moving on a fulcrum, or fixed point. The fulcrum may be somewhere between the force applied and the resistance offered (Class I lever); or it may be somewhere to one side of the resistance and the force, in that order (Class II lever); or it may be somewhere to one side of the force and the resistance, in that order (Class

III lever). The factor of leverage permits muscles to increase the speed of movement while decreasing the power; to increase the power while decreasing the speed; and to turn a movement into a new direction.

Attachments

Each skeletal muscle is attached to bone at two points one point, the origin, remains fixed, while the other, the insertion, is movable. The illustration on page 120 shows the sartorius muscle (of the left thigh) that extends from the hip to the upper foot. The sartorius traverses two joints; therefore, it can flex the leg at the knee, and it can also flex the thigh at the hip or rotate the thigh. This double action is not common, however, inasmuch as in most cases a muscle affects only a single joint. As a skeletal muscle contracts, the part attached to the bone at the origin moves very little or not at all, whereas the part attached to the bone at the insertion draws nearer to the origin. In this way, for example, the temporalis muscle, with a fixed origin, contracts to close the jaw. With certain muscles, either end can serve as the origin or as the insertion, depending on the type of movement.

Attachments of muscles to bones may be direct (here the connective tissue, or *fascia*, connects with the periosteum of the bone), or they may be indirect (here either the strong fibrous *tendons* or the broad sheets called *aponeuroses* connect with the bone). The tendon for certain muscles of the abdomen is shown in the center of the illustration on page 120. Note (in the lower part of the rectus sheath) the two openings of the inguinal canals, which provide a passage for the two (right and left) spermatic cords. Inguinal hernia (rupture) may occur in this region if the contents of the abdomen press against a weakened portion of the abdominal wall, propelling peritoneum and part of the intestine into the canal.

Classes of Skeletal Muscles

There are four classes of skeletal muscles: prime movers, antagonists, synergists, and fixators. A prime mover is any muscle that is responsible for a definite motion; for example, the latissimus dorsi muscle extends the upper arm. An antagonist is any muscle responsible for movement opposite to that of a prime mover; thus, the pectoralis major muscle flexes the upper arm and is therefore the antagonist of the latissimus dorsi muscle. A synergist is any muscle that aids the prime mover by keeping one joint steady while the prime mover applies force to a neighboring joint; thus, the wrist muscles keep the wrist immovable when the fingers are being flexed. A fixator is any muscle that keeps the bone at the origin steady while the prime mover

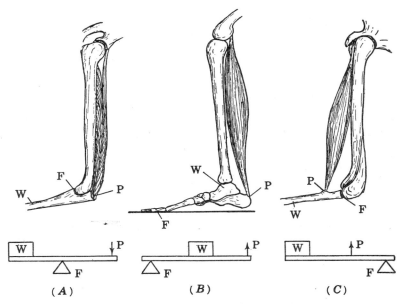

FIG. 15. Diagrams to suggest the relations between the three classes of levers and the actions of skeletal muscles. (A) First class lever, illustrated by the triceps muscle extending the arm at the elbow. (B) Second class lever, illustrated by the gastrocnemius muscle raising the weight of the body on the toes. (C) Third class lever, illustrated by the biceps muscle flexing the arm at the elbow. Abbreviations: F, fulcrum; P, power; W, weight. (From Gordon Alexander, *Biology,* College Outline Series.)

pulls away from it: thus, the biceps and triceps muscles act to keep the elbow in a fixed position.

Major Groups of Skeletal Muscles

The body has about 656 muscles (2 single, 327 pairs). Muscles account for about 42 per cent of body weight in males, about 36 per cent in females. The following table lists the principal groups of the skeletal muscles. (See the illustrations on pages 120–121.)

26 MUSCLES OF THE HEAD

Muscles of expression—e.g., corrugator: pulls eyebrow down; located below frontalis; origin, frontal bone; insertion, eyebrow and nose

Muscles of mastication—e.g., temporalis: closes jaw; located in temporal fossa of skull; origin, temporal bone; insertion, mandible

Muscles of the tongue—e.g., styloglossus: draws tongue backward or to side; located along front side of tongue surface; origin, temporal bone; insertion, sides of tongue

Muscles of the pharynx—e.g., stylopharyngeus: raises pharynx and larynx; located in pharyngeal wall; origin, temporal bone; insertion, lateral larynx wall and posterior part of larynx

Muscles of the soft palate—e.g., levator veli palatini: raises palate; located in dorsolateral part of soft palate; origin, temporal bone and auditory tube; insertion, soft palate

32 MUSCLES OF THE NECK

Muscles that move the head—e.g., splenius capitis: extends and rotates head; located across side of neck; origin, lower cervical and upper thoracic vertebrae; insertion, temporal bone and superior nuchal line

Muscles that move the hyoid and larynx—e.g., stylohyoideus: pulls hyoid up and backward; located in angle of mandible; origin, temporal bone (styloid process); insertion, hyoid bone (body)

Muscles that act on upper ribs—e.g., scalenus anterior: raises first two ribs or turns neck to side; located in side of neck below sternocleidomastoid muscle; origin, anterior tubercles of transverse processes of third to sixth cervical vertebrae; insertion, scalene tubercle of first rib

598 MUSCLES OF THE TRUNK AND EXTREMITIES

Muscles that move the vertical column—e.g., quadratus lumborum: extends spine or abducts trunk to side; located in posterior abdominal wall; origin, ilium and through lower lumbar vertebrae; insertion, twelfth rib and first four lumbar vertebrae

Muscles that move the scapula—e.g., levator scapulae: raises scapula; located in neck under trapezius muscle; origin, first four cervical vertebrae

Muscles of respiration—e.g., rectus abdominis: compresses abdomen, pulls thorax downward; located on each side of linea alba from sternum to pubis; origin, pubis; insertion, xiphoid cartilage, linea alba, pubic crest

Muscles that act on the humerus—e.g., deltoideus: abducts humerus, raises arm, rotates arm; located in shoulder, forming shoulder prominence; origin, clavicle, acromion, and spine of scapula; insertion, deltoid tuberosity of humerus

Muscles that act on the forearm—e.g., brachialis: flexes the forearm; located on anterior surface of humerus; origin, distal portion of humerus; insertion, coronoid process of ulna

Muscles that act on the hand and digits—e.g., extensor digitorum communis: extends wrist, fingers, forearm; located on posterior surface of arm; origin, humerus; insertion, dorsal surface of phalanges of fingers

Muscles of the pelvic outlet—e.g., coccygeus: flexes sacrum and coccyx, helps support pelvic organs; located between ischium and sacrum and coccyx; origin, ischium; insertion, sacrum and coccyx

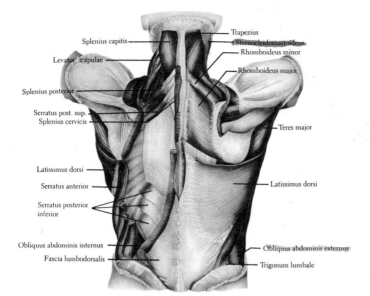

Fig. 16. Intermediate back muscles.

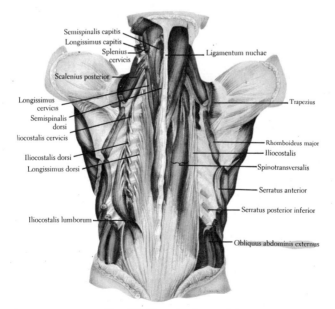

Fig. 17. Deep back muscles.

Muscles that act on the femur—e.g., pectineus: adducts and flexes femur; located on inner side of thigh; origin, crest of pubis; insertion, pectineal line of femur

Muscles that act on the leg—e.g., sartorius: flexes leg at knee, flexes thigh at hip, rotates thigh; located diagonally across surface of thigh; origin, anterior, superior spine of ilium; insertion, medial surface of tibia

Muscles that act on the foot and toes—e.g., gastrocnemius: extends foot, flexes leg at knee joint; located in superficial posterior portion of leg, forming calf; origin, femur; insertion, calcaneus by way of tendon of Achilles

DISORDERS OF MUSCLES AND TENDONS

Muscles generate motive power which is transmitted by tendons. If the force exceeds the permissible load or if it is applied too suddenly, injury (trauma) may result. The sheath covering the tendons may develop a painful inflammatory swelling (*tenosynovitis*); or tendons may actually be torn from their attachments to bones, and the tear may be accompanied by an audible snap and by the sensation of a sharp blow ("Charley horse").

Cramps are painful, sustained muscular contractions, possibly due to insufficient oxygen for the local blood stream.

Spasm is a term applied to involuntary contractions of muscles. Examples are the constrictions of intestinal muscles due to local irritation (colic); gallstone colic caused by passage of a stone along a gall duct; and spasms of the bronchioles in the lungs, as in hay fever and other allergies (and particularly in asthma).

Sprain is the result of an excessive stretching of the ligaments, tendons, or muscles. Muscle fibers or whole muscles may be ruptured by violent contractions. If such injuries are extensive, surgical repair may be required. In some cases healing may become a prolonged process.

A *hernia* (rupture) is a protrusion of a part from its normal location, resulting from a weakening of its supporting structures. Examples are the common inguinal hernia in the groin, occurring when intra-abdominal structures descend through the inguinal canal; umbilical hernia, occurring when these structures descend through the navel; and diaphragmatic hernia, occurring when they descend through the diaphragm.

In *tetanus* (lockjaw), caused by infection with the tetanus bacterium, muscles are locked in persisting contraction (tonic spasm).

In *epilepsy,* muscles contract and relax alternately (convulsions).

Progressive muscular dystrophy is characterized by destruction of muscle fibers. This disorder is hereditary, but the precise cause is unknown.

The loss of voluntary muscular movement may be a result of injury or disease of the brain or spinal cord. The destruction caused by a brain hemorrhage ("stroke," *apoplexy*) may involve the motor center controlling an arm or a leg, with a subsequent loss of motion (*paralysis*) of the corresponding limb. The virus of *infantile paralysis* attacks the gray matter of the spinal cord or brain. It has a predilection for motor cells in the gray matter of the spinal cord, causing partial or complete paralysis of the muscles under the control of the nerve cells involved. The ultimate consequence may be a wasting (atrophy) of part or all of the muscles affected, but the damage can often be alleviated by suitable treatment.

VI—THE NERVOUS SYSTEM

The millions of cells comprising the human body must work together harmoniously for the effective performance of organic functions. The primary function of the nervous system, the stimulus-response mechanism, is to ensure the coordinated, smooth operation of all parts of the body. Consciousness, feeling, memory, learning, and reactions to messages received by sense organs are also functions of the central nervous system.

The three divisions of the nervous system are the central, the peripheral, and the autonomic. The central nervous system consists of the brain and the spinal cord. It is protected by its location within the skull cavity and the spinal canal. The peripheral nervous system consists of the nervous structures outside the brain and spinal cord. The autonomic nervous system runs parallel to the spinal column from the neck to the pelvis. It consists of a chain of ganglia connected by nerve fibers. It is the "involuntary" nervous system; it controls organs of vital processes (heart action, respiration, digestion, excretion).

STRUCTURE AND FUNCTIONS OF NERVE TISSUE

Nerve stimuli may originate internally (e.g., from activity within the central nervous system, heart, and digestive organs) or externally (e.g., from light, heat, pressure). The resulting nerve impulses are transmitted by energy generated in the nerve fibers through which they pass. These impulses may be conducted along nervous tissues to sense organs, the spinal cord, the brain, or the end organs; or they may be conducted to muscles or glands. Thus they may cause the eye (a *sense* organ) to respond to light or they may stimulate a muscle (an *effector* organ) to contract so as to move a limb. (The term *receptor* has been variously used to denote a sense organ, a sensory nerve ending, a sensory neuron, or a single cell adapted to receive a specific type of stimulus.) The nerve tissues along which the nerve impulses travel consist of neurons and their supporting or connecting cells called *neuroglia*.

43

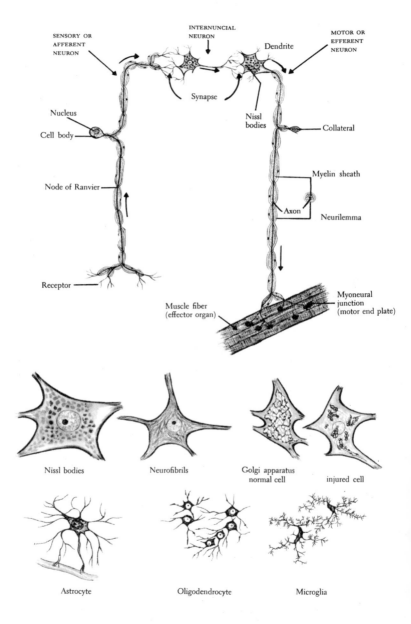

FIG. 18. Types of neurons.

Neurons

A typical neuron has a central cell body and one or more projections, the cell processes. The cell body consists of a large, spherical nucleus (usually with a large nucleolus and a small nucleolar satellite) and cytoplasm around the nucleus. The cell processes are of two kinds: dendrites—branching projections which conduct nerve impulses to the cell; and axons—some very short, some 3 feet or longer, which conduct nerve impulses away from the cell. There can be only one axon in a neuron, though it may give off several collaterals, but there may be one or many dendrites. Axons generally have one or more white, fatty (myelin) sheaths. A nerve impulse starts in a dendrite of a receptor (sensory nerve ending) and travels through the cell body and out of the axon. The impulse then crosses the contiguous boundary between axon and dendrite (the synapse) to contact the dendrite of the next neuron. It continues through the cell body and axon of the second neuron, then across the synapse to the dendrite of the third neuron, and so on in a continuous chain. In transmitting nerve impulses, however, the neuron is not restricted to a single route; it may conduct the impulse to several other neurons at one and the same time through its connections with them. While the nerve impulse usually is conducted from the axon end of each neuron, across the junction, or synapse, to the dendrite of the next neuron, once activated a nerve fiber can conduct equally well in either direction (antidromic conduction).

It should be noted that afferent neurons are those that conduct impulses from the sense organs to the spinal cord, brain, or end organs. Efferent neurons are those that conduct impulses from the central nervous system to effector organs. Efferent neurons may be motor, carrying impulses to voluntary muscles; secretory, carrying impulses to glands; accelerator, carrying impulses that stimulate the activity of visceral or cardiac muscles; or inhibitor, carrying impulses that retard or stop the activity of visceral or cardiac muscles. (Found only within the central nervous system is a third type of nervous tissue, the internuncial neurons, which carry nerve impulses from one neuron to other neurons, and no further.)

Nerve fibers are the groups of fibers which conduct the nerve impulse. They may consist of the axons of neurons or of certain dendrites (called axon-like dendrites because they resemble axons) found in the spinal nerves. There are four kinds of nerve fibers: the naked axon fibers (those without a sheath and found only in the central nervous system); the unmyelinated fibers (those with only an outer sheath called a neurilemma, especially numerous in the autonomic nervous system); the myelinated fibers (those with a thick, white sheath without an outer sheath, occurring in the central nervous system); and myelinated fibers with an outer sheath, found in the peripheral nervous system.

Neuroglia

The neuroglia form the supporting, interstitial tissue of the nervous system and include the following types of cells: ependyma, in the lining of the brain ventricles and the center portion of the spinal cord; neuroglia proper, or glia cells, found between the neurons in the brain and spinal cord; satellite or capsular cells, in sensory neurons of the peripheral ganglia (masses of nerve cells); and neurilemma, or sheaths of Schwann, around the peripheral processes of cranial and spinal nerves.

Nerves, Plexi, and Tracts

Nerves are the white cable-like structures (located outside the central nervous system) over which the nerve impulse travels in a manner that is similar to the way that electrical waves travel over electrical wires. A nerve consists of nerve fibers (grouped in bundles, or fasciculi), together with their blood vessels and lymphatic vessels and fiber coverings. The perineurium is the thin covering of a fasciculus, with thin strands (the endoneurium) extending among the nerve fibers; the epineurium, comprising the membrane that covers the nerve, contains blood vessels and adipose tissue, encloses the fasciculi, and contains the nervi nervorum, or sensory nerve fibers. Bundles of nerve fibers may be connected within a single nerve, or the fibers may divide into branches connecting with other nerves to form a nerve network, or plexus. Inside the spinal cord and brain, however, when the nerve fibers connect to form bundles, these are called tracts instead of nerves In the cord, ascending tracts carry afferent impulses to the brain, while descending tracts carry efferent impulses from the brain. In the brain, projection fibers connect the cerebral cortex and the brain stem or the spinal cord; commissural fibers connect both sides of the brain; and association fibers connect brain parts on the same side. Injury to a group of projection tracts (the internal capsule) of the brain may cause paralysis from hemorrhage (apoplexy or stroke).

Nerve Action

If a nerve in the peripheral system is injured or cut, the fibers in its distal portion are severed from the cell bodies and degenerate. But a new axon may gradually grow and restore the nerve structure; this process of regeneration is aided by bringing the two cut ends of a severed nerve close together. Conversely, in very painful conditions such as trigeminal neuralgia, effective treatment consists of blocking the nerve (in this case, the trifacial nerve) by removing the Gasserian ganglion so that the parts of the nerve will remain separated. Regeneration does not occur among nerve structures in the central nervous system, in which, however, other nerve structures may sometimes take over the functions of the injured ones.

The brain and parts of the spinal cord contain masses of gray nerve fibers and cell bodies which act as integrating centers for organizing nerve impulses and thus make possible the higher mental processes of reasoning, or judging, and understanding. The brain and the cord also contain white matter, the groups of nerve fibers (with a fatty, myelin sheath) which serve mainly as conductors of nerve impulses.

It is clear, then, that nerve tissue possesses the properties of irritability (the ability to respond to a stimulus), conductivity (the ability to conduct nerve impulses), and integration (the ability to organize and regulate nerve impulses). Like heart muscle and single striated muscle fibers, the neuron follows the all-or-none principle, inasmuch as it reacts at its maximum to any stimulus that is strong enough to be effective. To become an effective stimulus, a chemical, mechanical, neural, electrical, thermal, or other force must have a minimal strength, it must occur suddenly, and it must continue its action for a minimal period of time at a minimal rate of occurrence. A weaker stimulus may be longer than a stronger one, but its longer duration will be of no avail if it is below minimal intensity. Furthermore, as in the case of muscle tissue, a more powerful stimulus affects more fibers and in this way produces a greater flow of nerve impulses. The nerve also resembles muscle tissue in that it will be unable to react unless it can rest briefly between stimuli. Unlike muscle tissue, however, nerve fibers are not subject to fatigue, although toxic substances or the lack of oxygen may impede their activity. Nerve impulses can be blocked by the application of extreme cold, by pressure on the nerve (e.g., crushing the phrenic nerve to stop movements of the diaphragm in cases of intractable tuberculosis), and by electrical or chemical applications. (In general anesthesia, the anesthetics cause loss of consciousness by interfering with nerve functions.)

All nerve impulses are fundamentally alike and can be regarded in the same way as electrical or other types of waves. The nerve impulses differ from one another primarily as to the areas of the body which they activate. Thus, light rays entering the eye stimulate the optic nerve to transmit the nerve impulses to the cortex of the brain and in this manner produce the sensation of vision; but sound waves ordinarily affect the acoustic nerve, not the optic nerve, and transmit nerve impulses to the temporal lobe of the brain, producing the sensation of hearing. It is the impact upon the specialized type of nerve structure and brain area that causes the sensation.

Reflex Action

The nerve mechanism responsible for most activities of the organism is called reflex action. A simple three-neuron type of reflex action may be illustrated as follows. A stimulus, for example an acid, applied to the skin affects the receptor consisting of the endings of afferent neurons in the skin. The resulting nerve impulse is carried along a neuron to the spinal cord, thence through the dendrite, cell body, and axon of the neuron to the dendrite of a connecting neuron in the gray portion of the cord, where the impulse enters an efferent or motor neuron. From the axon of the motor neuron the impulse is carried into a spinal nerve connecting with a muscle which contracts in response to the impulse. Reflex actions of this kind are automatic, specific, and designed to perform a definite, useful function. Reflexes can become highly complex, involving multiple stimuli, many neuron pathways or arcs, and a number of responses. Some reflexes seem to be inborn or of extremely early development,

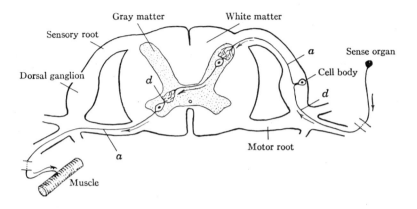

FIG. 19. Relations between spinal cord and spinal nerves. Three neurons, constituting a simple reflex arc, are represented. The direction of the nerve impulse through them is indicated by arrows. Abbreviations: a, axon; d, dendron. (From Gordon Alexander, *Biology*, College Outline Series.)

such as chewing, swallowing, defecation, and the like; others are learned from repeated experience—for example, after numerous repetitions of stimuli and responses the sound of a dinner bell (the stimulus) causes the saliva in the mouth to flow (the response) in automatic, reflex action even though there may be no food available. (This learned action is called a conditional reflex.)

Certain disorders of the nervous system may be indicated by the failure of normal reflexes to function. Among the important reflexes checked by physicians for diagnosis are the knee jerk or patellar reflex (the leg extends in response to tapping the patellar tendon), the Achilles reflex (the foot extends in response to tapping the tendon of Achilles), the corneal reflex (the eye closes in response to touching the cornea), the pupillar reflex (the pupil of the eye constricts in response to a bright light), and the Babinski reflex (the toes extend in response to stroking the sole of the foot).

THE CENTRAL NERVOUS SYSTEM

The central nervous system, with its two main divisions (the brain and the spinal cord), is the control center which regulates the activities of the body. The brain lies within the cranial cavity and connects at its lowest portion (the medulla oblongata) with the spinal cord. The spinal cord lies within the vertebral canal of the spinal column and extends downward to the second lumbar vertebra.

The Brain

The three main divisions of the brain are the brain stem, the cerebellum, and the cerebrum. Subdivisions of the brain stem are the medulla oblongata (the lowest portion of the brain), the pons, and the midbrain. Behind the medulla and the pons is the cerebellum, a large structure connected to them and to the midbrain. Superior to the cerebellum is the cerebrum, the largest brain structure.

THE MEDULLA OBLONGATA

The medulla oblongata is an extension of the spinal cord, a triangular enlargement about 3 cm. long which contains vital nerve centers for regulating the heart beat, the diameter of arteries and veins, the rate of respiration, and swallowing and other reflex actions. Through the medulla oblongata the nerve fibers extend upward and downward between the spinal cord and other parts of the brain. As they pass through this structure, some nerve fibers cross over from one side of the spinal cord to the other; it is by this means that the left side of the brain controls the right side of the body, while the right side of the brain controls the left side of the body. The medulla oblongata also contains nuclei of eight cranial nerves. So vital is this part of the brain stem that injury or disease affecting it is apt to have fatal consequences

THE PONS

The pons is an oval-shaped structure above the medulla oblongata. It serves as a central bridge for nerve fiber tracts conducting nerve impulses between the medulla oblongata and the cerebral cortex and cerebellum—the higher brain centers. It also has nuclei of important cranial nerves—the trigeminal or trifacial (5th), abducens (6th), and facial (7th) nerves and branches of the acoustic (8th) nerve.

THE MIDBRAIN

Above the pons is the midbrain, which connects lower to higher brain centers, contains nuclei of important cranial nerves, and serves as a conducting center for acoustic, tactile, and visual reflexes. It is a center for the regulation of body posture and equilibrium.

THE CEREBELLUM

The cerebellum is the second largest division of the brain. It has two hemispheres and a middle section (the vermis) shaped like a coiled worm. It consists of external gray matter and internal white matter, the latter being called arbor vitae because of its branched treelike appearance. It coordinates muscular movements initiated by cerebral action, controlling the continued contractions and relaxations of muscles so that the various groups of muscles work together instead of acting in a chaotic manner. It keeps muscles in a healthy condition of partial contraction (tonus) and functions to maintain equilibrium and good posture. Severe injury to the cerebellum upsets muscular coordination, particularly noticeable in the affected individual's attempt to perform skilled activities requiring integration or careful balance.

THE DIENCEPHALON

Between the midbrain of the stem and the cerebrum is a structure called the tween-brain, or diencephalon. It consists of several parts: the thalamus, a center through which nearly all afferent nerve impulses travel on their way to the cerebral cortex; the epithalamus, which contains olfactory centers and the pineal body (see page 150); the subthalamus, which regulates muscles of emotional expression; and the very important hypothalamus, with its centers for control of body temperature. of emotions that affect the heart beat and blood pressure, of appetite and fat metabolism, and of sexual reflexes. The master gland of the body, the hypophysis or pituitary gland, is located at the base of the hypothalamus (see page 148); so, too, are the optic chiasma, a band of nerve fibers connecting with the optic nerves and optic tracts, and the mammillary bodies which function in the conduction of olfactory impulses.

THE CEREBRUM

The cerebrum, by far the largest portion of the brain, covers all the other parts. It consists of two hemispheres separated

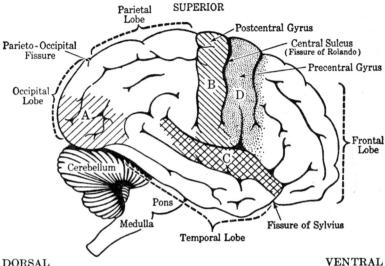

SUPERIOR

Parietal Lobe

Parieto-Occipital Fissure

Occipital Lobe

Postcentral Gyrus

Central Sulcus (Fissure of Rolando)

Precentral Gyrus

Cerebellum

Frontal Lobe

Pons

Medulla

Fissure of Sylvius

Temporal Lobe

DORSAL   VENTRAL

FIG. 20. Right cerebral hemisphere. Lateral view, showing important fissures, lobes, and projection centers of cortex, medulla and pons, and cerebellum. The dotted area (D) represents roughly the origin of main efferent tracts conducting impulses from the cortex to lower co-ordination centers; crosshatched areas (A, B, and C) represent projection areas for vision, somesthesis, and audition, respectively. (From Fryer, Henry, and Sparks, *General Psychology,* College Outline Series.)

vertically by a groove but connected horizontally by a thick white band of nerve fibers (the corpus callosum) and two smaller bands (commissures). The surface of the cerebrum, arranged in a large number of folds (convolutions or gyri), is the cortex, which consists of gray matter. The inner white matter, interspersed with a few nuclei of gray matter, is enclosed by the cortex. The folds are separated by deep furrows (sulci) and also by shallow furrows (fissures).

In this way each hemisphere is divided by the fissures and sulci into five parts, or lobes: the frontal lobe, or anterior part; the parietal lobe, or superior-lateral part; the temporal lobe, or inferior-lateral part; the occipital lobe, or posterior part; and the insula (central lobe, or island of Reil), inferior to the frontal lobe. The chief motor areas of the cerebral cortex are in the

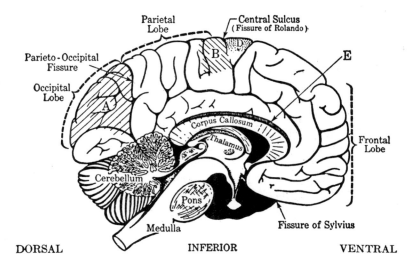

DORSAL INFERIOR VENTRAL

FIG. 21. Left cerebral hemisphere. Mesial view, showing thalamus, corpus callosum, and part of the projection area for olfaction and gustation (E) The primary area for smell and taste, not shown, is the uncus, situated in the hippocampal convolution on the inferior surface of the temporal lobe. (From Fryer, Henry, and Sparks, *General Psychology*, College Outline Series.)

frontal lobe; the neurons here extend down the spinal cord and connect with axons of neurons which stimulate skeletal muscles. (It will be recalled that, since the axons of such neurons cross to the opposite side of the spinal cord, each hemisphere of the cerebrum controls muscles on the opposite side of the body.) The chief sensory areas of the cortex are in the parietal lobe, controlling sensations of touch, pressure, heat, cold, position, and pain. But control of visual sensations resides in the occipital lobe, and injury to it may cause blindness even though the optic nerve and visual organs remain healthy. Control of acoustic (auditory) and olfactory sensations is attributed to the temporal lobe, injury to which may cause auditory and olfactory disorders.

In addition to the motor and sensory areas, the cerebral cortex has association areas, which play a large role in coordinating the higher mental functions, such as memory and learning,

emotional reactions, and understanding or judgment. Association areas constitute the major portion of the cortex. One such
area is Broca's area (in the left inferior frontal fold) which acts
as a speech-control center. Another is Wernicke's center (in the
temporal-occipital fold) for understanding speech. Injury to
these two areas may cause aphasia (in which there is either loss
of ability to understand spoken words or a loss of ability to
speak and write words).

Each hemisphere of the cerebrum has in its interior portion
some basal ganglia (masses of gray cells), which seem to function as centers for the coordination of voluntary muscle movements. Virus infection (encephalitis) or arteriosclerosis of the
basal ganglia may cause Parkinson's disease and rheumatic fever
may initiate the acquired form of St. Vitus' dance or chorea (conditions exhibiting uncontrollable tremors of the limbs).

Coverings (Meninges) of the Brain and Cord

Three membranes (arranged in layers) cover the brain and
the spinal cord, supplementing the protection afforded by the
cranial bones and the vertebrae. These membranes, called
meninges, are: (1) the dura mater, a heavy, elastic outer covering, with several folds or extensions separating the cerebral
hemispheres; (2) the arachnoid, a thin, weblike, protective membrane separated from the dura mater by a tiny space (the sub-
dural space); and (3) the pia mater, a transparent, innermost
membrane containing blood vessels supplying the brain. Another
space (the subarachnoid space) separates the arachnoid from
the pia mater. In the spinal cord the three membranes and spaces
are continued, but differ sharply in size from those in the brain. Inflammation of the brain coverings (meningitis) usually affects
the arachnoid and the pia mater.

The brain has four cavities (ventricles), the first two of which
are in the cerebral hemispheres, while the third is a slit between
the thalami and connects with the fourth cavity which is mainly
in the medulla oblongata. The cavities are filled with a watery,
alkaline fluid (cerebrospinal fluid) that is formed in vascular
tissue in the ventricles, flows through the subarachnoid space,
and acts as a shock absorber for the brain and spinal cord. This
fluid, constantly absorbed and reformed, also provides some
glucose, proteins, and other nutrients for the nervous system.

The Spinal Cord

The spinal cord, consisting of 31 continuous segments, is a cylindrical structure with an inner core of gray matter and an outer substance of white matter containing supporting cells (neuroglia) and blood vessels. The gray core contains neuroglia, neurons, and networks of nerve fibers. It is H-shaped and has in its center a canal extending through the length of the cord. The white fibers conduct afferent nerve impulses from the peripheral nerves of the body to the brain and, conversely, efferent nerve impulses from the brain to the nerves in the lower cord. The gray matter provides centers for connections between the afferent and efferent nerve impulses. The cord is a little longer in men than in women, averaging about 42 cm. in length. It weighs about 30 grams. It is the main cable for nerve-impulse conduction, vital to all types of sensation and movement.

The bundles of white fibers in the cord are known as fiber tracts. The ascending tracts (afferent fibers) conduct the nerve impulses to the brain; the descending tracts (efferent fibers) conduct impulses to the lower cord. The various tracts conduct sensory impulses for touch, muscular movement, equilibrium, and pain and temperature, each tract specializing in its own kind of conduction. A good example of the ascending tracts is the spinotectal tract. Its cells cross over in the spinal cord and continue upward into the midbrain, conducting nerve impulses that produce sensations of pain, touch, and temperature. An example of the descending tracts is the vestibulospinal tract. It runs from a vestibular nucleus nerve of the medulla oblongata downward to a front column of the spinal cord, near its surface. This tract conducts nerve impulses that affect muscle tension and equilibrium. Infection or injury in ascending tracts causes the loss of sensory perception; infection or injury in descending tracts causes loss of power of movement. The serious consequences of a spinal fracture often arise from the fact that pressure by dislocated vertebrae may injure the cord.

THE PERIPHERAL NERVOUS SYSTEM

The peripheral nervous system consists of nerve structures outside the brain and spinal cord. It connects the central nervous system with the periphery of the body and conducts nerve impulses between them. It includes the 12 pairs of cranial nerves (and a newly discovered 13th nerve reaching to the nasal septum); the 31 pairs of spinal nerves; and certain nerves, ganglia, and plexi which are concerned with involuntary muscular movements of body organs. The last-named constitute a functional system called the autonomic nervous system; it has two divisions—the sympathetic division, with its ganglia alongside the spine, and the parasympathetic division, with its terminal ganglia at those internal organs affected by nerve impulses.

Cranial Nerves

Some of the cranial nerves are only sensory, but the majority are mixed, including both sensory and motor nerve fibers. The cranial nerves are attached to the base of the cranium and exit through openings (foramina) therein; the cell bodies of sensory (afferent) fibers are outside the brain, whereas the motor fibers are inside the nuclei of the brain. The 12 pairs of cranial nerves are as follows:

  I Olfactory (smell)—sensory nerves from the olfactory bulb to epithelial organs for the sense of smell
 II Optic (vision)—sensory nerves which form the optic chiasma and extend to the retina of the eye
III Oculomotor (eye movements)—mixed nerves from the midbrain to eye muscles and eyelid muscles
 IV Trochlear (eye movements)—mixed nerves from the midbrain to the superior oblique muscles of the eye
  V Trigeminal (mastication)—mixed nerves (in three branches) from the pons to the lacrimal gland and muscles of mastication; also relays sensations from nasal membranes, skin of face, and upper and lower lips
 VI Abducens (eye muscle movement)—mixed nerves from the pons to the lateral rectus muscle of the eye
VII Facial (taste, muscle sense)—mixed nerves from the pons to the face, neck, jaw, and scalp muscles and tongue buds; also affects submaxillary and sublingual glands
VIII Acoustic (hearing, sense of balance)—sensory nerves from the pons and medulla oblongata to the cochlea, the vestibule, and the semicircular canals of the ear
 IX Glossopharyngeal (swallowing, taste, cutaneous sensations of the ear)—mixed nerves from the medulla oblongata to muscles of the pharynx, tongue, palatine tonsils, parotid gland
  X Vagus (hunger, pain, respiratory reflexes, swallowing, actions of internal organs)—mixed nerves from the medulla oblongata to the pharynx, larynx, trachea, bronchi, lungs, aortic arch, internal organs

XI Spinal accessory (movements of the neck, shoulder, and soft palate)—
    motor nerves from the medulla oblongata to the muscles of the
    neck, shoulder, soft palate
XII Hypoglossal (muscular movements of the tongue)—mixed nerves
    from the medulla oblongata to the tongue muscles

It should be noted that all excepting the first two cranial
nerves originate in the brain stem.   Nerve IV is the smallest, V the
largest, X the longest of the cranial nerves.

Spinal Nerves

The 31 pairs of spinal nerves, arising from the cord, consist
of the following pairs: 8 cervical, 12 thoracic, 5 lumbar, 5 sacral,
1 coccygeal.   All excepting the first cervical emerge horizontally
through openings between the vertebrae; the first cervical passes
between the atlas and the occipital bone.   Each nerve is attached
to the spinal cord by two roots, anterior and posterior, which
unite as a nerve trunk a short distance away from the cord.

In the chest region, each pair of spinal nerves is specialized
for a particular part of the body.   But elsewhere, adjacent anterior branches of the nerves subdivide to form networks or plexi:
cervical, brachial, lumbosacral, and coccygeal.   Branches of the
cervical plexus (derived from the first four cervical nerves)
reach the skin of the shoulder, neck, and head, and muscles
such as the trapezius; phrenic branches go to the diaphragm.
(If the cord is severed in an accident above the phrenic nerve,
the impulses cannot reach the diaphragm and breathing stops.
Infantile paralysis may also paralyze the phrenic nerve, neces-
sitating use of an "iron lung.")   The brachial plexus of nerve
fibers, formed by lower cervical and the first thoracic nerves,
lies in the armpit; it goes to the arm and hand muscles and skin.
The lumbosacral plexus has similar functions in connection with
the lumbar region of the back, the thigh and leg, buttocks and
foot, rectum and genitalia.   (The sciatic nerve in this plexus is
the largest in the body and is subject to neuralgia, or sciatica.)
The coccygeal plexus, with its sacral nerves, goes to the skin
area around the coccyx.

THE AUTONOMIC NERVOUS SYSTEM

The autonomic nervous system activates the involuntary
smooth and cardiac muscles and glands throughout the body.

It serves the vital organ systems which function automatically—digestive, circulatory, respiratory, urinary, reproductive, and endocrine. Its nerves have two types of axons: white, fibrous so-called first-order neurons in the brain and spinal cord; and gray, so-called second-order neurons outside the brain and cord —very widely distributed fibers affecting cutaneous blood vessels and glands, as well as internal organs.

The two divisions (sympathetic and parasympathetic) of the autonomic nervous system oppose each other in function, thus maintaining balanced activity in the body mechanisms. In the brain, the hypothalamus, cerebral cortex, and medulla oblongata control the two divisions and coordinate their action so that they increase or decrease the activity of body organs as needed. Thus, the parasympathetic fibers to the heart slow down the heart beat, whereas the sympathetic fibers accelerate it. The parasympathetic fibers stimulate salivary and digestive secretions, whereas the sympathetic fibers inhibit them. The former constrict the bronchi; the latter dilate them. In a similar fashion, these two subdivisions of the autonomic nervous system regulate micturition and bladder responses, the respiratory rate, the heart rate, blood flow and blood pressure, body temperature, digestive, liver, and intestinal functions, and the endocrine glands.

DISORDERS OF THE NERVOUS SYSTEM

Injury to a sensory nerve stops the passage of impulses from the periphery to the central nervous system. The peripheral area served by the injured nerve (for example, a patch of skin) is no longer able to send messages to the brain. Consequently, the area appears senseless (anesthetic). Injury to a motor nerve stops the passage of impulses conveying "commands" from the brain to a muscle (paralysis). Damage to a cranial nerve disrupts the functioning of the corresponding organ. For example, damage to the eighth (auditory) nerve by accident or disease causes deafness on the side affected; disease of the seventh (facial) nerve results in a paralysis (Bell's palsy) of some of the facial muscles, with dropping of the angle of the mouth on the side affected.

Section (cutting) of a peripheral nerve separates it from its nerve cell in the spinal cord. As a result, the lower (distal) part of the nerve fiber degenerates (dies) and becomes absorbed, leaving only the neurilemma sheath. In the process of restoration (regeneration), fibrils grow out from the proximal end (nearer to the nerve cell) of the cut nerve and penetrate into the distal neurilemma sheath. Complete restoration of the longer nerves serving the lower parts of the legs requires many months. Nerves situated within the central nervous system are unable to regenerate because they lack a neurilemma sheath. The optic nerve is among the nerves subject to this deficiency.

The common headache is attributed to a great variety of disturbances. Headaches may be caused by generalized (systemic) disorders, such as infectious fevers (measles, typhoid, influenza) or high blood pressure. They may have a local origin in the nasal sinuses or in congestion or spasm of blood vessels in the brain (e.g., in migraine); or they may be caused by inflammation of the meninges (as in meningitis).

A blow against the head may entail only minor discomfort, or it may involve serious injuries accompanied by unconsciousness (concussion). In fact, injury or disease that puts out of commission any constituent of a reflex arc disrupts the transmission of sensory impulses to the central nervous system or leads to a blockage of the resulting motor impulse ordinarily sent to the periphery. Thus, the destruction of a pathway in the spinal cord by the organism causing syphilis stops the patellar reflex (knee jerk).

VII—THE SENSE ORGANS

Through the action of sense organs, the individual is made aware of himself and his world. His experience is based in the first instance upon a fourfold process: a stimulus affects a nerve structure; the impulse contacts and activates a sense organ (receptor organ, such as the eye); the impulses aroused in the sense organ travel to the brain; and one or more structures in the brain interpret the impulses as a feeling or sensation. The feeling or sensation in the brain is often projected to some other part of the body (as in the sensation of pain in a limb) or to the point of stimulation outside the body (as in sight of a distant object).

It is worth noting that pain in the skin is generally recognized as such, but pain arising from stimuli among internal organs is frequently referred to some surface region of the body. Thus, pain in the heart may be felt as pain in the left arm, liver pain as pain in the right shoulder, stomach pain as pain in the upper back, kidney pain as pain in the lower abdomen or in the thigh, pain in the area of an infected tooth as pain in the maxillary sinus or the ear. Sometimes, emotional disturbances may cause pain to be felt in an organ that is perfectly sound and healthy. A variety of limitations may restrict the range and dependability of sensations. It appears that environmental forces must possess special characteristics before they can arouse reactions in sense organs, such as those of the skin. Radioactivity can kill a man or change the genes in reproductive cells, yet is not detectable by the unaided senses.

Sensations have been classified as exteroceptive, proprioceptive, and interoceptive. Exteroceptive sensations arise from stimuli outside the body, which affect receptors in the skin and special receptors in the ear and eye. Proprioceptive sensations arise from stimuli in muscles, tendons, and joints, which affect receptors in these structures and in the semicircular canals of the ear. Interoceptive sensations arise from stimuli, such as pressure and chemicals within the body, which affect receptors in the internal organs and special receptors in the tongue and nose. The following paragraphs discuss the three classes of receptors.

SENSE ORGANS OF THE SKIN

Stimulation of the skin has widespread effects throughout the body. So vital is this function that some animals will die prematurely if they are not licked by the mother's tongue. The licking process initiates nerve impulses which travel to the internal organs and stimulate their activity and development. A similar mechanism operates in the human body. This is one reason that breast-fed babies seem to fare better than bottle-fed babies; the latter must compensate for a lack of stimulating nerve impulses normally aroused during breast feeding.

Sensations originating in the skin include touch and pressure, heat and cold, and pain. The receptors, consisting of free nerve endings in the skin, range in number from about 16,000 for heat to 4 million or more for pain.

SENSE ORGANS OF HEARING

The three divisions of the ear are the external ear, the middle ear, and the inner ear. Each division contains structures whose functions are necessary for normal hearing (the auditory or acoustic sense) or for equilibrium (the sense of balance). The illustrations on pages 63 and 137 show the main structures in each division of the ear. (The semicircular canals function as proprioceptive receptors, which will be discussed later in connection with sense organs of equilibrium.)

The External Ear

Note in the illustration the external ear, with its pinna (auricle) of cartilage and muscles surrounding the opening (the external auditory meatus) of the ear canal extending to the middle ear. The tympanic membrane separates the canal from the middle ear tympanic cavity. The handle of one ear bone, the malleus, is attached to the inner surface of the membrane, which is vibrated by sound waves reaching it through the canal.

The Middle Ear

Internal to the membrane are the bony promontory and three small bones of the tympanic cavity. The bones are the hammer (malleus), anvil (incus), and stirrup (stapes)—i.e., the auditory ossicles—each connected with the others by joints. The ossicles are activated by the small tensor tympani muscle (tensor muscle of the ear drum) and the stapedius muscle (which is attached to the stapes and acts upon it). These structures constitute the middle ear. In this region there are several openings: one leads from the external ear and is covered by the tympanic membrane; the stapes inserts into another opening, the oval window (fenestra ovalis); a third opening is the round window (fenestra rotunda); a fourth opening leads into the mastoid process and sinuses; and a fifth opening leads into the auditory (Eustachian) tube which terminates at the back of the nose. The auditory tube has a bony section, enclosed by the temporal bone, and a cartilaginous section extending into the pharynx. To enable the ear to receive sound waves with the greatest fidelity, it is necessary to maintain equal air pressure on both sides of the ear drum. This optimum condition prevails as long as the external ear on one side and the Eustachian tube on the other side are in free communication with the outside air.

The Inner Ear

The inner ear has two passageways: the bony (osseous) labyrinth and the membranous labyrinth. The bony labyrinth contains the vestibule (an oval middle portion); three bony semicircular canals; and two bony chambers of the cochlea. The snail-shaped cochlea has three chambers filled with perilymph fluid—two bony chambers and one membranous chamber—and several membranes; on its basilar membrane rests a spiral organ (the organ of Corti) with hair cells that transmit auditory impulses. The bony labyrinth encloses the membranous labyrinth. The latter has two subdivisions—the utricle and the saccule—as well as the third, membranous chamber of the cochlea, and three semicircular ducts, each with an ampulla, or prominence, at one end. The three semicircular canals lie in planes at right angles to each other to facilitate effective perception of changes in the position of the head. The three ducts contain a fluid (origin unknown) called endolymph and, being within the bony labyrinth, are themselves immersed in its perilymph, which is derived from the cerebrospinal fluid. (Note that the three semicircular canals of the bony labyrinth contain perilymph, not endolymph.)

Steps in Hearing

A complex series of steps is required for normal hearing. Sound waves collected by the auricle enter the external ear canal. The waves strike the tympanic membrane and cause it to vibrate. The vibrations are transmitted to the hammer (malleus) and the anvil (incus), and the motion of the anvil moves the stirrup (stapes). The movement of the stirrup against the oval window

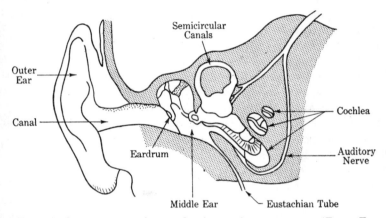

FIG. 22. Cross section of ear, showing major structures. (From Fryer, Henry, and Sparks, *General Psychology,* College Outline Series.)

transmits the vibrations to the perilymph fluid in the vestibular chamber (scala vestibuli) and to the tympanic chamber (scala tympani) of the cochlea. The important basilar membrane, which separates these two chambers, is set in motion by the disturbed perilymph fluid. The motion of the basilar membrane, in turn, disturbs the endolymph fluid in the third chamber—the membranous duct area of the cochlea. In the duct the free ends of the hair cells of the organ of Corti (the auditory receptors and primary sense organs of hearing) are stimulated by the motion of the fluid. The hairs bend against another membrane (the tectorial membrane) and send impulses along the cochlear nerve (the auditory branch of the stato-acoustic or 8th cranial nerve) to the brain. Interpretations of the impulses by the brain constitute hearing.

Defective hearing may result from injury or disease affecting the major structures or connecting pathways of the ear. Rupture or thickening of the tympanic membrane, stiffening of the ossicles, adhesion of the footplate in the stapes, or infection or tissue blockage in the Eustachian tube may prevent normal transmission of sound waves. Injury to the cochlea or to the cochlear nerve may restrict the range or sensitivity of hearing. Brain abscesses or skull injuries obviously may severely limit or destroy the hearing function. A common disorder is otitis, or inflammation, particularly of the middle ear (otitis media); the infection may spread from the upper respiratory tract, through the Eustachian tube to the middle ear, and then all the way to the mastoid air cells, resulting in mastoiditis. Another common disturbance is tinnitus, or ringing in the ears, which may be caused by excessive wax secretions, inflammation of the cochlea, or the use of drugs, such as quinine.

Although air is the normal conductor of sound waves, acting upon the ear bones, it is possible to hear sound vibrations conducted through various other bones of the skull to the cochlear fluids of the inner ear. Certain deficiencies of hearing can be counteracted to some extent by instruments making use of alternative routes of bone conduction.

SENSE ORGANS OF VISION

The chief structures for the sense of vision are the eyeball, with its cavities, three coats or tunics, and refracting media; the accessory structures of the eye, including the eyebrows, eyelids, conjunctiva, lacrimal apparatus, and ocular muscles; and the orbits, or skull cavities, housing the eyes and certain bones, openings, fascia, blood vessels, and nerves.

The Eyeball

The outside coat of the eyeball is the fibrous sclera—the white of the eye—which has eye muscles attached to it and also has an opening for the optic nerve on its posterior surface. The front part of the sclera extends outward in a convex curve and constitutes the transparent cornea. (See illustrations, page 138.)

The middle coat of the eyeball includes the choroid, the ciliary body, and the iris. The choroid is a dark, brown membrane just beyond the sclera. The ciliary body is a thickened extension of the choroid; it has a ring, many ridges or processes, and a muscle; and a suspensory ligament from its ridges supports the elastic capsule that encloses the lens of the eye. The ciliary muscle changes the shape of the lens and thus influences the refraction of light rays. The iris is a colored, round disc continuous with the ciliary body and containing in its center the open space called the pupil. The muscles of the iris contract and relax, reducing or increasing the size of the pupil, and thus regulating the amount of light allowed to pass to the lens. Between the lens (which is directly behind the pupil) and the iris there is a small posterior chamber, while between the iris and the cornea is a larger anterior chamber. Both chambers are filled

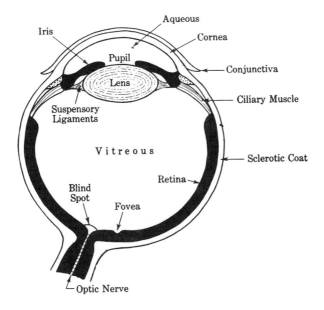

FIG. 23. Cross section of eye, showing major structures. (From Fryer, Henry, and Sparks, *General Psychology*, College Outline Series.)

with alkaline, watery fluid (aqueous humor) which flows into the canal of Schlemm and thence to the veins of the eye.

The innermost coat of the eyeball consists of the retina, a nerve membrane with three layers of neurons and processes. One layer includes the rods and cones that function as the receptors of light rays reaching them through the outer layers. The rods, numbering perhaps 100 million, contain the pigment rhodopsin, which is decomposed by light and activates them so that they function in dim light. The cones function mainly in connection with bright light and color perception In the center of the back part of the retina is the macula lutea, or yellow spot, with its fovea centralis, where only cones are to be found; this is the place of clearest vision. About 3 mm. nearer to the nose there is a white circular area called the optic disc (or blind spot because no rods or cones are present). Nerve fibers from all parts of the retina converge to this area to form the optic nerve, which pierces the sclera accompanied by the central artery and vein. The optic nerve then passes through the optic channel into the middle cranium where it meets and joins its fellow nerve (from the opposite eye) and shortly reaches the thalamus and midbrain. Injury or disease affecting the optic nerve of one eye may interfere with the function of only the single eye, but lesions in the higher routes to the brain may cause half-blindness in both eyes because some nerve fibers cross over from one side of the visual pathway to the other side.

The large space between the lens and the retina (four-fifths of the total area of the eye) is filled with a jelly-like material called the vitreous body.

Accessory Structures of the Eye

The accessory structures of the eye have important functions The eyebrows consist of thickened skin with numerous hairs and help protect the eyes. The upper and lower eyelids consist of thin skin, a circular muscle for closing the lids, stiff tarsal plates (connective tissue) and tarsal glands. The free edges of the eyelids carry the eyelashes and lubricating glands.

Tears are produced by the lacrimal glands under the eyelid and are discharged through ducts at the edges of the lids. The tears accumulate in the lacrimal lake at the nasal corner (inner canthus). They are drained from this area into the nose by ducts starting in a small reddish prominence (the caruncle) at the inner canthus. Tears contain salt, mucin (for lubrication) and lysozyme.

The conjunctiva is a mucous membrane lining the eyelids and the sclera. It is frequently subject to infections (conjunctivitis), as, for instance, in common colds. When the resulting excessive outpouring of tears cannot be drained into the inflamed nasal cavity, the fluid accumulates (i.e., the eyes "water").

The Orbits

The orbit of the eye is a cone-shaped cavity or bony socket for the eyeball. The boundaries of each of the two orbits are formed by the frontal, zygomatic, maxillary, sphenoid, ethmoid, lacrimal, and palatine bones. The apex of the cone lies toward the posterior portion in which are located the optic foramen (opening), for the optic nerve and ophthalmic artery, and the superior orbital fissure for various nerves controlling the ocular muscles. (There are seven extraocular muscles, six of which move the eyeball, while the seventh raises the upper eyelid.) Fibrous sheets and muscles within the orbit bind the structures and protect them; fascia and ligaments help to regulate eye movements. Large quantities of fatty tissue are normally present. (In starvation, loss of fat may result in a shrunken appearance of the eyes.) The ophthalmic artery supplies blood for the eyeball, muscles, and glands. The central artery, a branch of the ophthalmic, extends through the center of the optic nerve to the retina. The nerves of the orbit include (1) the oculomotor, trochlear, and abducens nerves—for impulses to the muscles and to the brain; (2) a branch (ophthalmic) of the trigeminal (5th facial) nerve—a sensory branch for eye structures and surrounding skin areas; and (3) a number of autonomic nerves for control of the iris and ciliary body.

The Mechanics of Vision

The function of seeing depends upon light rays which enter the eye and, passing through the lens into the retina, affect the rods and cones which send impulses along the optic nerve to the brain.

The light rays traverse the cornea and aqueous humor, then are refracted by the lens. The bending of the rays produces an inverted image on the retina, but the brain reverses the image during interpretation so that it is again perceived upright. The lens is pulled by the ciliary muscle to change its shape as needed so that the light rays will focus properly on the retina even though the object being viewed moves farther away from or nearer to the eye. Thus, to view near objects, the ciliary muscle contracts to make the lens more spherical and bend the light rays sufficiently for them to focus on the retina. If the lens has lost much of its elasticity, however, as in the presbyopia of old age, corrective glasses may have to be worn. In binocular vision (vision with two eyes) the light rays from an object normally strike corresponding points on the two retinas. The two somewhat differing images are interpreted by the brain as a single, fused image.

If muscular defects or differences in the curvatures of the lenses in the two eyes prevent the eyeballs from converging properly, one eye will tend to turn inward or outward. In "crosseye" the two eyes converge excessively, and in "wall-eye" they diverge excessively. In nearsightedness (myopia) the eyeball is too deep and causes light to focus in front of the retina; concave glasses spread the light rays before they reach the lens and thus correct the condition. In farsightedness (hyperopia) the light rays focus behind the retina; convex glasses will converge the rays on the retina. In astigmatism the cornea or the lens is irregularly curved so that the horizontal and vertical rays focus at different points on the retina, producing indistinct vision. Cylindrical glasses are worn to correct this condition.

SENSE ORGANS OF EQUILIBRIUM

When muscles or tendons stretch, their nerve receptors transmit impulses to the central nervous system which enable the brain to judge body position and balance. These sensations are known as the kinesthetic or proprioceptive sensations. They enable us to maintain erect posture, normal muscle tension (tonus), judgments of weight and pressure or resistance, and coordinated movements of the body. In certain disorders of the nervous system, as in locomotor ataxia, the nerve impulses from stretching muscles fail to reach the brain; then the individual cannot judge his position or balance correctly and is therefore unable to walk in a normal manner. Many physical activities of everyday living involve judgments of weight and equilibrium and to this extent depend upon the action of proprioceptive sense organs.

The sense organs (receptors) for skeletal muscles consist of nerve endings around certain muscle fibers (intrafusal fibers) and are called neuromuscular spindles. The sense organs for tendons are called neurotendinous spindles. The comparable nerve endings in ligaments are called Pacinian corpuscles (pressure receptors found in deep layers of the skin of the feet and

1ands, as well as in the ligaments); these receptors are activated
)y movements of the joints.

Another type of sense organ for equilibrium are the highly
specialized semicircular ducts of the inner ear. In fact, awareness
of body position depends primarily upon the functions performed
oy the semicircular ducts and also those performed by the utricle
and saccule of the inner ear. Head movements stir up the fluids
in the utricle and saccule, bending the hairs and sending nerve
impulses along the vestibular branch (vestibular nerve) of the
stato-acoustic nerve to the brain. The resulting reflex actions
keep the body in its normal position of static equilibrium. If the
body moves out of position, fluids in the cochlear ducts bend the
hairs in the crista (a small elevation) of the ampulla, sending
information to the medulla oblongata and cerebellum. In this
way, the brain judges body position; it then transmits motor
impulses to the eyes and skeletal muscles (effectors), which adjust
the body posture and movements accordingly. The sense of
vision helps to maintain equilibrium through direct retinal reflexes and also through the substitution of visual for proprioceptive information (e.g., when communication between the lower
part of the body and the brain is cut off by disease).

Motion sickness may arise from overstimulation of the fluids
of the ear; the effects can be largely counteracted by the
use of drugs, such as dramamine. Frequent spells of dizziness
and chronic disturbances of equilibrium may arise from abnormalities of the inner ear, brain lesions, and ocular, intestinal, or
cardiac disease.

RECEPTORS FOR INTERNAL ORGANS

The receptors serving internal organs consist of (1) the free
nerve endings in the mucous membranes of the organs (these
nerve endings stimulate sensations necessary for the normal
functioning of the digestive, respiratory, circulatory, urinary,
and reproductive systems—e.g., sensations of fatigue, hunger,
thirst, and pain); and (2) specialized receptors, principally those
of the tongue and nose—for sensations of taste and smell.

Barrel-shaped taste buds on the tongue (and also on the soft
palate, pharynx, and larynx) are receptors for taste stimuli
The mechanism whereby solutions of food and liquids initiate
impulses in the taste buds is unknown. Taste sensations, pro·

duced when the impulses reach the cerebral cortex, may be salty
sour, bitter, or sweet. Taste buds seem to be selective in their
reactions. For example, those at the sides of the tongue transmit
impulses for sour tastes, those at the tip for sweet tastes, those
at the sides and tip for salty tastes, and those at the root for
bitter tastes. But individuals differ considerably in their taste
reactions; furthermore, the sequence of tastes changes their
character, and some foods counteract the tastes normally associated with other foods (e.g., lemon juice can be masked by
adding enough sugar). Acids are generally sour, chlorides salt
alkaloids and bile salts bitter, and organic products (e.g., sugar)
sweet. Some food flavors are mixtures of two or more basic
tastes; others represent mixtures of tastes and odors.

Gases entering the nasal cavity stimulate the small receptors
(olfactory cells) in the sides, roof, and wall of the nose. The
impulses travel to the olfactory bulb and eventually reach the
olfactory cortex in the brain. Ordinarily, deeper breathing draws
the air gases in more rapidly, with magnified results. Odors are
intermingled with taste sensations and are often hard to differentiate; the taste of an onion is really dependent upon its
odor, its characteristic flavor disappearing if the nose is closed.
The individual may adjust gradually to offensive odors and
therefore remain unaware of a slowly increasing volume of gas.
The intensity of strong odors may often diminish as if the
receptors were becoming fatigued and were no longer able to
react vigorously. Some chemicals (for instance, the dangerous
carbon monoxide gas) escape detection because they have no
effect upon the olfactory mechanisms of the nervous system.
The fact that smell plays an important role in taste perception
explains why food is tasteless to a person suffering from a head
cold.

DISORDERS OF THE SENSE ORGANS

The preservation of life depends upon prompt reactions to danger and
upon constant adaptations to environmental changes. These reactions and
adaptations highlight the role of the sense organs. Thus, the approach
of an attack or other menacing situation, whether perceived by means of
sight, hearing, or smell, triggers chain reactions (in the central nervous
system and in the endocrine glands) that prepare the individual for "fight
or flight." The heart beats more forcefully, breathing becomes deeper, and
more sugar is poured into the blood to sustain the anticipated muscular
effort.

Pain sometimes has a beneficial function, as demonstrated dramatically in the case histories of serious afflictions. In their early stages, heart disease, cancer, and tuberculosis, however, too often fail to indicate their onset by means of discomfort; in such instances, treatment may not be started at the most favorable time. Ordinarily the sensation of pain enables the individual to counteract danger and induces him to seek help.

Pain arising among internal organs may be felt in some surface region of the body. The mechanism of referred pain starts with transmission of a stimulus from a diseased organ to the brain (cerebral cortex), where it is projected to another area often at a considerable distance from the affected organ. Pain originating in a diseased heart (angina pectoris) may be felt in the upper chest, left arm, or left jaw. Similarly, gallbladder disease may cause pain in the right shoulder instead of in the right upper abdomen.

The proprioceptive sense informs us about the relative positions of the parts of our body. Thus, without looking at our arm, we know when it has been raised to point upward or lowered to point downward. The proprioceptive sense enables us to stand and to walk. If the proprioceptive impulses from the lower limbs are prevented from reaching the brain by destruction of the connecting nerves (as in locomotor ataxia), the victim no longer knows the position of his feet, and to walk he is forced to lift his feet higher than necessary. If such a person is prevented by darkness or blindness from using his eyes to gauge his position in space, he will be unable to stand erect but will sway (the Romberg Test measures this lack of coordination). In fact, a patient may be unaware that he has contracted this disease until he falls forward unexpectedly, perhaps while washing his face.

Various defects of vision have been noted in our discussion of the mechanics of vision (page 68). Blindness may be due to loss of transparency in the refracting media of the cornea and the lens. Corneal opacities may be the result of infection (e.g., gonorrheal conjunctivitis contracted at birth) or of scars. Often vision can be restored by grafting a normal cornea from another eye to replace the diseased cornea. Opacities of the lens may be the result of injury (traumatic cataract) or of ageing (senile cataract). In many of these cases, vision can be reestablished by surgical removal of the obstructing lens. Detachment of the retina and blocking (thrombosis) of the central artery of the retina are other frequent causes of blindness. These conditions may be caused by injury or disease. Another serious disorder, glaucoma, is characterized by an increase in the pressure within the eye, which ultimately leads to blindness through compression of the retina and the optic nerve. Glaucoma is often due to blocking of the outflow tract, the canal of Schlemm. Surgical removal of part of the iris may save vision by fashioning a new outlet for the intraocular fluid.

Exophthalmos is the term denoting protrusion of the eyeballs, a condition usually resulting from overactivity of the thyroid gland (see page 165).

Styes and cysts are common disorders of the eyes. A stye (hordeolum) is an inflammation of a sebaceous gland at the edge of an eyelid. A cyst filled with a hard core (a chalazion) may arise from blockage of a tarsal (Meibomian) gland in the eyelid.

VIII—THE CIRCULATORY SYSTEM

Blood is the principal fluid of the heart and circulatory system. Other body fluids include tissue fluid in the spaces between cells; lymph fluid of organs such as the tonsils, spleen, and thymus; cerebrospinal fluid in the brain and spinal cord; synovial fluid in the joint cavities; aqueous humor of the eye; and special fluids of the ear. The latter four types of fluid have been referred to in preceding discussions. Blood and lymph will be considered in this section.

BLOOD

Blood consists of liquid (plasma) and tissue elements (corpuscles). Slightly more than half of the blood volume is plasma, 91 per cent of which is water, 8 per cent proteins, and the rest acids, glucose, gases, hormones, antibodies, and enzymes. The corpuscles include red cells (erythrocytes), white cells (leucocytes), and tiny plates (platelets or thrombocytes). The red blood cells number about 35 trillion (4.5 to 5 million per cu. mm.) in the average person and contain hemoglobin pigment which unites with oxygen that is carried to the body tissues. The white blood cells (about 6,000 per cu. mm.) include a variety of cells differing in structure, shape, and functions. These cells destroy bacteria, help to repair tissue, and may be the source of protective substances, such as antibodies. The tiny platelets (numbering about 300,000 to 400,000 per cu. mm.) release a blood-clotting substance and help to seal leaks in the capillaries (the network of microscopic vessels transporting blood from small arteries to veins). It is worth noting that the body obtains vitamin K from greenleaf vegetables or the secretions of intestinal bacteria; this vitamin is needed by the liver in order to provide a substance (prothrombin) required for blood-clotting.

Since numerous illnesses have specific, known effects upon the number of blood cells of the different types, a blood count may disclose the nature of an ailment. Thus, anemia is a decrease in the normal number of red cells or of the normal amount of hemoglobin in each cell; this condition may be due to malnutrition. Increases in the number of certain white cells may be caused by infectious diseases, allergies, or intestinal parasites; decreases may be associated with typhoid fever, toxic substances, influenza, or tuberculosis. Leukemia may cause a marked increase in white blood cells together with a decrease in red blood cells. In hemophilia, the blood platelets fail to function normally, and the blood does not clot normally.

Blood performs essential functions: nutritive—carrying food to body tissues; respiratory—carrying oxygen from lungs to cells, carbon dioxide from cells to lungs; excretory—carrying waste products from cells to excretory organs; protective—carrying antibodies and bacteria-killing substances (phagocytes) to all parts of the body; and regulatory—distributing hormones and other chemicals, maintaining normal body temperature by getting rid of internal heat, and keeping a balance between the internal supplies of water and other fluids.

In blood deficiency, as in hemorrhage, shock, or disease, whole blood or its plasma may be injected by transfusion. Since the characteristics of the clotting substance differ among the four types of blood (O, A, B, and AB), care in transfusion must be taken. It is dangerous to use group O individuals as donors, even though their blood is often satisfactory for emergency transfusions. Even people with the so-called "universal type" (AB) may encounter difficulty in some cases if they are given transfusions of blood of another type. There is also a special (Rh) clotting substance in the blood of most people, but if their blood is given to persons without such a factor in their own blood, the recipients develop antagonistic substances which will cause their blood to clot in subsequent transfusions. Blood plasma, as distinct from whole blood, can be used without involving such difficulties.

Clots can form within blood vessels as a result of injury or infection. These clots (thrombi) may remain in one vessel and be slowly absorbed, or they may be carried through the blood stream to a distant artery, shutting off its blood supply. The latter result has dangerous consequences when a clot lodges in some smaller artery supplying blood to a vital organ, such as the brain, heart, or lungs

Hemorrhage is excessive loss of blood through the blood vessels to the outside of the body or within the body cavities. It reduces the number of red blood cells and thereby the amount of oxygen available; it lowers blood volume and blood pressure; it speeds up the rate of heart action; and it diminishes the force of the beat. The body reacts by starting clotting action, constricting the blood vessels, withdrawing fluids from the tissues and contracting the spleen to circulate reserve blood in an attempt to replace the blood constituents lost. The application of heat stimulates the platelets to release more of their clotting substance, and the application of cold constricts the blood vessels; thus, both heat and cold can be used to reduce hemorrhage.

THE HEART

The heart is a muscular organ of interconnected, branching fibers, located between the lungs, with about two-thirds of its area to the left of the midline of the body, its upper portion or base at the level of the second rib, and its lower portion or apex pointing downward and to the left resting on the diaphragm on the level of the fifth rib. It is enclosed by a white fibrous sac, the pericardium; the sac has two layers between which is a lubricating fluid facilitating movement of the heart as it contracts and expands. The inner layer of the sac forms the outer lining of the heart and is called the epicardium. The heart wall has a middle layer, the myocardium, consisting of thick bands of muscular tissue; and it has a third layer, the endocardium, a thin, single layer of flat cells covering the heart valves and lining the cavities.

The heart has two upper chambers (the left and the right atria or auricles) and two lower chambers (the left and right ventricles). On the outside of the heart can be seen a groove on each side, separating the atria from the ventricles. On the inside a septum (partition) separates the two atria, and another septum (the interventricular septum) separates the two ventricles. The ventricles are larger than the atria and have thicker walls needed for pumping the blood against the pressure in the arteries; this feature is particularly noticeable in the left ventricle, which sends blood throughout the body, excepting the lungs. The right ventricle serves only the lungs.

The heart has four valves. These allow blood to flow in only one direction. The mitral (bicuspid) valve on the left side and the tricuspid valve on the right side are in the openings between the atria and the ventricles, allowing the blood ejected by the atria to flow into the ventricles. As the ventricles contract, the pressure of the blood flow against the flaps (cusps) closes them to prevent backflow and directs the blood stream into the aorta and pulmonary artery. The valves are kept in place by attached fibrous cords connected with the papillary muscles. Similarly, the semilunar valves in the openings of the aorta (the largest artery in the body) and of the pulmonary artery close to prevent the blood from flowing back into the heart when the ventricles relax after completing their contraction. If heart valves become deformed by inflammation and scarring, as in rheumatic fever, the blood may leak back through them in the wrong direction. In another condition, mitral stenosis, the mitral valve grows narrower and the blood flow is obstructed. The heart tries to compensate for this interference by pumping blood more forcibly and faster, causing heart muscles to grow larger and the heart chambers to dilate. In such a condition, strenuous activity may become impossible because the heart muscles cannot overcome the added heavy load imposed by the abnormal valve This condition leads to "heart failure," as manifested by shortness of breath (dyspnea) and by the accumulation of excessive fluids (edema) in the lungs, liver, and lower limbs. With further deterioration of the heart muscle, dyspnea and edema may accompany moderate or slight activity and may occur even during bed rest.

The heart beat consists of the alternate contractions and relaxations of the atria and ventricles. The beat is heard in a stethoscope as two sounds—lub-dub—the first, longer and lower sound resulting from closure of the bicuspid and tricuspid valves and contraction of the ventricles, the shorter and snapping sound resulting from closure of the semilunar valves. The pumping action is one of contraction (systole) and relaxation (diastole), followed by a brief rest interval, and its rhythm requires a balance in the supply of calcium, sodium, and potassium in the heart muscle. The heart beats normally about 70 times per minute.

BLOOD CIRCULATION

Blood circulates in a double circuit, one called pulmonary (supplying only the lungs), the other systemic (supplying the rest of the body). In the pulmonary circuit, as the right ventricle contracts, blood is forced into the pulmonary artery and thence is transported to the lungs, where it gives off carbon dioxide and unites with oxygen. It is then carried back in the pulmonary veins to the left atrium. In the systemic circulation, the left atrium contracts so that blood flows past the bicuspid valve into the left ventricle which pumps it into the aorta, then in arteries and arterioles to the capillaries of the tissues throughout the body. From the tissues the blood returns via the capillaries to

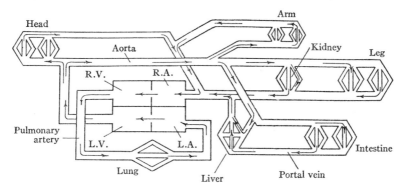

Fɪɢ. 24. Blood flow. (From Gordon Alexander, *Biology*, College Outline Series.)

venules, then to veins leading into the superior and inferior vena cava and the right atrium. Here it begins its first, pulmonary, circuit again with the contraction of the right atrium and right ventricle. Note that arteries carry blood from the heart, veins to the heart.

The heart muscle requires a constant blood supply for its own nutrition and oxygen needs. This supply is furnished by the two coronary arteries (right and left) which originate in the first portion of the aorta. They send branches to all parts of the heart. Because every one of these branches serves only a limited area of tissue (functioning as a "terminal artery"), there are only minor connections (anastomoses) with neighboring arteries. The great and middle cardiac veins return the blood to the right atrium via the coronary sinus.

Inadequacy of the coronary blood supply gives rise to chest

pains (angina pectoris). The final outcome, if the deterioration is progressive, may be a "heart attack." This condition (coronary occlusion or thrombosis) is caused by blocking (clotting) of a branch of a coronary artery. Since the coronary arteries are of the terminal type, without sizable connections to other arteries, the blood supply of the muscle segment fed by the clotted artery stops completely. The result is destruction (necrosis) of the affected area. If the patient survives the acute phase of the condition, a firm scar will replace the damaged tissue and, in many cases, a good recovery will occur.

Nerve impulses reach the heart from the medulla oblongata along the middle cervical (accelerator) and vagus (depressor) nerves. Fibers of these nerves extend to special neuromuscular tissue in two nodes and two bundles in the heart. These nodes are the sinoatrial or SA node in the right atrium and the atrioventricular or AV node in the interatrial septum. These neuromuscular tissues are important regulators of the heart rate. Impulses from the SA node spread out to cause the atrium to contract; the impulses then continue to the AV node, the starting point of the AV bundle, which sends right and left branches to activate the ventricles. If impulses are blocked as a consequence of disease in this conduction system, the ventricle may contract at a very slow rate independently (heart block).

Although the cardiac centers in the brain (i.e., in the medulla oblongata) exercise control over the heart, sensory nerve impulses in other parts of the body may affect the heart rate. Thus, a sudden emotional reaction may increase the rate, while other stimuli, such as a blow in the abdominal region (for example, against the solar plexus), may reduce it. Overloading of the circulation beyond the danger point may lead to bursting of arteries. To guard against such a contingency, special nerve receptors are built into the circulation to serve as safety valves. These structures are situated in the first portion of the aorta and on the carotid arteries in the neck (carotid sinuses). The receptors are highly sensitive to minute variations of blood pressure and pulse rate. If these factors rise above the optimum level, depressor impulses are sent to the brain, slowing the heart rate and lowering the blood pressure through dilatation of peripheral blood vessels. In the reverse contingency, with excessive drop of blood pressure and slowing of the heart rate (e.g., in fainting), accelerator impulses are sent to the brain, restoring optimum conditions.

Chemicals may affect heart action profoundly, as seen when there is a lack of oxygen or an excess of carbon dioxide. Digitalis slows the heart, as do muscarine, pilocarpine, and choline. Atropine and thyroxin increase the rate; a rise in body temperature, accompanying fever or physical exertion, has a similar effect.

As the blood enters the aorta from the heart, it starts a pressure wave along the arteries. This wave is the pulse; it travels much faster than the blood and arrives at the wrist in about a tenth of a second. The arterial pulse can be felt at the wrist, over the temporal artery, at the facial artery crossing the mandible, at the side of the neck, inside the biceps muscle, at the femoral artery crossing the pelvic bone, at the instep, and at the popliteal artery posterior to the knee.

Blood presses against the walls of the blood vessels, reaching a maximum in the aorta, and gradually decreases on its way along the arteries, capillaries, and veins. The pressure in arteries when the ventricles contract is called systolic pressure, averaging about 120 for young adults; 150 or over may indicate hypertension. The pressure during ventricular relaxation is called diastolic pressure, averaging about 80. Cardiac muscle action also produces electrical charges which reach the body surface and can be detected and analyzed by use of an electrocardiograph which records waves correlated with atrial and ventricular contractions. Disturbances in heart action are often reflected by variations in the recorded waves.

SYSTEMIC CIRCUITS

The circuits listed below indicate the main routes of blood on its journeys to and from all parts of the body.

Circuit through the Heart

aorta --- coronary arteries --- heart wall capillaries --- cardiac veins --- coronary sinus --- right atrium

Circuit through the Upper Extremity

ascending aorta --- aortic arch --- brachiocephalic (innominate) artery on the right --- subclavian artery --- axillary artery --- brachial artery --- smaller arteries --- tissue capillaries --- smaller veins --- basilic or cephalic veins --- axillary veins --- subclavian vein --- brachiocephalic (innominate) vein --- superior vena cava --- right atrium

Circuits through the Neck and Head

(A) ascending aorta --- aortic arch --- brachiocephalic artery --- subclavian artery --- vertebral artery --- basilar artery --- circle of Willis --- smaller arteries and arterioles to cranial capillaries, venous sinuses, internal jugular vein --- brachiocephalic vein --- superior vena cava --- right atrium
(B) from brachiocephalic artery through carotid arteries to external jugular vein, subclavian vein and brachiocephalic vein to superior vena cava and right atrium
(C) from carotid arteries to cerebral arteries

Circuits through Digestive Organs

(A) ascending aorta --- aortic arch --- thoracic aorta --- abdominal aorta --- celiac artery --- hepatic artery or splenic artery --- smaller arteries --- spleen --- pancreas --- splenic vein --- portal vein --- liver --- hepatic veins --- inferior vena cava --- right atrium
(B) ascending aorta --- aortic arch --- thoracic aorta --- abdominal aorta --- mesenteric arteries --- upper and lower intestines --- mesenteric veins --- portal vein --- liver --- hepatic veins --- inferior vena cava --- right atrium

Circuit through the Kidney

ascending aorta --- aortic arch --- thoracic aorta --- abdominal aorta --- renal artery --- smaller arteries in kidney --- afferent artery to glomerulus of kidney --- efferent artery from glomerulus --- renal tubules --- small veins in kidney --- renal vein --- inferior vena cava --- right atrium

Circuits through the Lower Extremities

(A) ascending aorta --- aortic arch --- thoracic aorta --- abdominal aorta --- common iliac and external iliac arteries --- femoral artery --- popliteal or posterior tibial arteries --- smaller arteries and arterioles --- tissue capillaries --- saphenous veins or popliteal vein --- femoral vein --- external iliac vein --- common iliac vein --- inferior vena cava --- right atrium
(B) from common iliac artery to internal iliac artery --- smaller arteries --- tissue capillaries --- internal iliac vein --- common iliac vein --- inferior vena cava --- right atrium

Note that the veins include (in addition to the pulmonary and systemic circuits) a portal system of circulation serving the intestines, spleen, pancreas, and gallbladder. Blood flows from these organs along the portal vein to the liver, where the vein subdivides into two trunks and then into small vessels called sinusoids that transmit blood from the liver to the sublobular veins, into the hepatic veins, and to the inferior vena cava. The portal system includes veins carrying blood from the spleen, pancreas, stomach, esophagus, and gallbladder. (See diagrams on pages 125–131.)

FETAL CIRCULATION

In the fetus, the lungs and digestive tract do not function. The fetal blood flows through umbilical arteries to the placenta, which is the mother's organ that provides nutrition and oxygen for the fetus. Within the placenta the blood passes through the capillaries, is oxygenated, and returns to the fetus via the umbilical vein, thence to the inferior vena cava or to the liver and hepatic veins. The blood in the right atrium of the fetus passes through an opening (foramen ovale) in the wall separating the atria and continues directly to the left atrium, then either through the left ventricle and aorta or through a duct (ductus arteriosus) connecting the pulmonary arteries with the aorta. The foramen ovale closes at birth, the ductus arteriosus begins to close, and the umbilical vein becomes a round ligament of the liver. If the ductus arteriosus of the child fails to close sufficiently, however, unoxygenated blood gets through directly to the left atrium instead of passing through the lungs first for oxygen—the result being the "blue baby," reflecting the lack of oxygen. (Note that no blood passes from the mother's circulation to that of the fetus.)

LYMPH

Tissue fluids carry nutritive substances to tissue cells of the body and take from them their waste products. The fluids which enter lymph vessels and ducts are called lymph. These fluids are not pumped through the ducts. They are propelled by differences in capillary pressure, muscle action, intestinal movements, and respiratory and other sources of pressure. Lymph flows through the lymph vessels and ducts into the blood stream. The two main ducts are the thoracic duct (extending from the abdomen through the diaphragm, thorax, and neck into the left subclavian vein) and the right lymphatic duct (a short duct ending in the right subclavian vein). The lymph ducts resemble veins but have numerous valves and glands (nodes) which filter the lymph, clearing it of bacteria, arresting carbon particles and malignant cells, and manufacture white blood cells (lymphocytes and monocytes). Groups of these filtering centers are in the head, face, and neck, thoracic region, armpits, lower limbs and groins, and pelvic and abdominal regions. Inadequate drainage of lymph results in swelling (edema) in the tissue spaces. Infections and malignant cells may spread along lymph vessels.

The chief lymphoid organs are the spleen, tonsils, and thymus. The spleen is the largest (about 200 gm. in weight, 12 cm. long, and 8 cm. wide) and is located below the left side of the diaphragm and behind the fundus of the stomach. It forms blood cells, filters injurious substances from the blood, stores iron for use in the manufacture of hemoglobin, stores blood, produces a bile pigment (bilirubin), and furnishes antibodies against bacteria and parasites. In anemia, malaria, or leukemia, the spleen is enlarged. The tonsils consist of lymphoid organs in the pharyngeal walls. They manufacture lymphocytes. The thymus gland (see page 153) is situated in the chest, above and in front of the heart.

DISORDERS OF THE CIRCULATORY SYSTEM

Recent advances in the treatment of circulatory disorders constitute an outstanding achievement. High blood pressure (hypertension), one of the most common afflictions, can now be controlled by means of a variety of measures and medications. Tests have been devised for the diagnosis of one type of hypertension caused by a tumor of the adrenal gland (pheochromocytoma). Relief from hypertension contributes to efficiency and longevity by reducing strain on the heart and other vital structures.

Structural defects of the heart may be congenital, or they may be the result of infections. Congenital abnormalities include gaps in the atrial or interventricular septa, failure of the ductus arteriosus to close at birth, and transposition of certain structures. Infection by bacteria, including that causing "rheumatic" damage, may result in imperfect closure (leaking) or imperfect opening (obstruction, stenosis) of heart valves. Often such defects are compatible with a long and active span of life. In some cases however, medical treatment or operative correction by heart surgery are necessary.

IX—THE RESPIRATORY SYSTEM

All organisms exchange gases with their environment. Even the single-celled ameba obtains oxygen as well as nutrients (and discharges carbon dioxide) through the cell membrane. To obtain oxygen and discharge waste products, higher organisms require a special respiratory apparatus.

EXTERNAL RESPIRATION

The human body takes in oxygen and discharges carbon dioxide by means of breathing, or external respiration. This process consists of inspiration (to take air into the lungs) and expiration (to expel air from the lungs). The inspired air passes through the nasal chambers, pharynx, larynx, trachea, right and left bronchi, and, finally, the alveoli (air sacs) of the lungs. By diffusion the red blood cells, coursing through the lungs, take in oxygen from the air and discharge carbon dioxide into it. The expired carbon dioxide returns via the same passageways to the outside. The pharynx is a passageway for food as well as air.

It should be noted that air is not drawn into the lungs by the mere force of inspiration alone; instead, the diaphragm (which is actually a great, dome-shaped muscle separating the chest from the abdominal cavity) and the chest muscles contract, increasing the size of the chest cavity (thorax), and in this way reduce the air pressure in the lungs, the primary organs of respiration. In addition, raising the sternum and ribs also helps to enlarge the chest cavity. Air flows to areas where the pressure is below the atmospheric level; consequently, these mechanisms cause an influx of air into the lungs. In expiration, the diaphragm and muscles relax so that the chest wall returns to its original position, pressure increases, and the thorax expels the air. Expiration may be aided by a number of muscles which act to increase the pressure and magnify the effect. Since the passage of air over the vocal cords causes them to vibrate and thus produce sounds (for which the nasal cavities provide resonance chambers), the function of speech is closely associated with that of respiration.

INTERNAL RESPIRATION

Within the body cells, in contrast to the interaction of blood and air in the lungs, a reverse process occurs. Here the circulating blood gives off oxygen to the tissues and takes carbon dioxide from them. The oxygen in the tissue cells combines with other substances which are repeatedly broken down into simpler oxygen-absorbing elements until only carbon dioxide and water remain in the tissues. This chemical change (oxidation) releases energy to the tissues for use in bodily activities. The exchange of gases between the blood and the body cells is called internal (or cellular) respiration. Some tissues, such as the muscles and glands, which use up a great deal of energy, especially in strenuous activity, discharge more carbon dioxide and require large quantities of oxygen. (Oxygen cannot be stored in the body but must constantly be replenished through the mechanism of blood circulation.)

THE NOSE

The nasal cavity (divided by the nasal septum into right and left passages called fossae) lies between the cranial cavity and the roof of the mouth. The anterior portion is formed by the nasal and frontal bones; in the middle portion, by the cribriform plate of the ethmoid bone; and in the posterior portion, by parts of the palatine, sphenoid, and vomer bones. The vomer and the perpendicular plate of the ethmoid form the nasal septum. In the middle portion of each lateral wall are three bony projections (the nasal conchae or turbinates) which divide each nasal cavity into three passageways—the superior, middle, and inferior meatuses. A mucous membrane lines this respiratory region.

In the area of the middle and inferior meatuses are numerous veins. Infection here may swell the membranes, causing nasal congestion (as in the common cold or in allergic reactions), and injury, heart failure, or hypertension may force blood to accumulate in the veins and result in nosebleed. Normally, it is the mucous membrane in the nasal cavity that protects the lungs by warming, moistening, and partially filtering the inspired air. Under the mucous membrane is a basement membrane, a layer of cells below which is connective tissue. Seromucous glands in the connective tissue furnish the secretions that moisten the nasal surfaces. The upper portion of the nasal cavity is the olfactory region; here the mucous membrane has receptors for the sense of smell.

THE THROAT

The pharynx, or throat, is a vertical, muscular, tubular structure about 5 inches long extending from the base of the skull down to the esophagus (gullet) and is divided into three parts: the nasopharynx, behind the nose and posterior and superior to the soft palate; the oropharynx, behind the mouth and between the levels of the soft palate and the epiglottis; and the laryngopharynx, behind the larynx and extending downward to the esophagus. The nasopharynx, which connects with the nasal cavity through the two posterior nares, has openings in its lateral wall to the auditory tubes (leading to the ears) and a lymphatic mass (the pharyngeal tonsil) on its posterior wall. The soft palate, separating the upper two divisions of the pharynx, is an arch-shaped membranous sheet covered with a mucous membrane and connected anteriorly to the hard palate. The opening (fauces) of the arch of the soft palate extends from the mouth into the oropharynx; and the two pillars of the arch (called pillars of the fauces) are on each side of the palatine tonsils, the troublesome organs removed by a tonsillectomy. The laryngopharynx, the bottom division of the throat, connects with the larynx through a triangular opening in its anterior wall behind the epiglottis and also narrows as it extends downward to join the esophagus.

THE LARYNX

The larynx, or "voice box," a tubular structure connecting the pharynx and the trachea, consists of nine cartilages joined by an elastic membrane. The triangular thyroid cartilage, or "Adam's apple," consists of two connected broad plates (laminae) with two posterior projections (superior and inferior cornua). Another of the nine cartilages is the epiglottis, which during swallowing forms a lid over the opening into the larynx to prevent the entrance of food into the larynx. Within the walls of the laryngeal cavity are two pairs of folds. one pair, the vocal folds, or true vocal cords, consist of white fibrous bands that stand out on the lateral walls and enclose the vocal ligaments and vocal

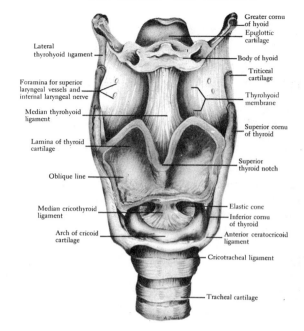

Greater cornu
of hyoid
Epiglottic
cartilage
Body of hyoid
Triticeal
cartilage
Thyrohyoid
membrane
Superior cornu
of thyroid
Superior
thyroid notch
Elastic cone
Inferior cornu
of thyroid
Anterior ceratocricoid
ligament
Cricotracheal ligament
Tracheal cartilage

Lateral
thyrohyoid ligament
Foramina for superior
laryngeal vessels and
internal laryngeal nerve
Median thyrohyoid
ligament
Lamina of thyroid
cartilage
Oblique line
Median cricothyroid
ligament
Arch of cricoid
cartilage

Fig. 25. The larynx.

muscle; the other pair above these, the ventricular folds, or false vocal cords, do not affect sound production. The glottis is the space between the true vocal cords.

The larynx has two groups of muscles: extrinsic muscles for over-all movement, as in swallowing; and intrinsic muscles which open and close the glottis during respiration, close the glottis in swallowing, and regulate tension of the vocal cords for production of sounds.

THE WINDPIPE

The trachea, or windpipe, is a tubular structure of smooth muscle located in front of the esophagus and supported by 16 to 20 C-shaped cartilage rings. It extends downward from the larynx (at the level of the sixth cervical vertebra) into the thorax, then bifurcates into two branches—the right and left bronchi leading to the lungs. The division into two channels occurs on the level of the fifth thoracic vertebra. The tissue comprising the trachea consists of four layers: the mucosa, or

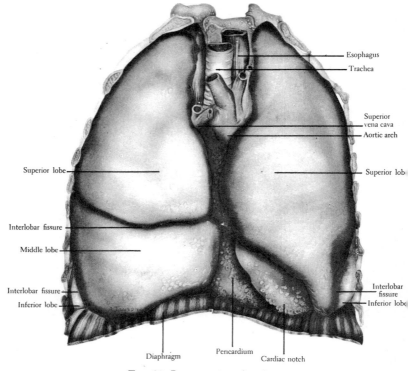

FIG. 26. Lungs and pericardium.

innermost layer of stratified epithelium, the submucosa, connective tissue containing numerous tubular glands which secrete mucus; the cartilage layer, enclosing smooth muscles between its ends; and the adventitia, a dense connective tissue with elastic fibers continuous with the surrounding connective tissue.

The trachea constitutes the main passageway through which air from the nasal chambers, pharynx, and larynx flows on its route to the bronchi and lungs. Obstructions often find their way into this broad channel; they may impede the flow of air, sometimes to such an extent that tracheotomy (an operation to open the trachea) becomes necessary to prevent asphyxiation.

THE BRONCHI

The two primary bronchi (the branches into which the trachea divides) extend into the right and left lungs. The right bronchus, about 1 inch long, is wider than the left and almost in a straight line with the trachea; the longer, narrower, left bronchus lies in a more horizontal position, and, consequently, aspirated foreign bodies tend to lodge more frequently in the right bronchus. The bronchi have cartilaginous rings and ciliated mucous linings similar to those of the trachea.

Immediately on entering the lung, each bronchus divides into smaller (secondary) bronchi, with two in the left and three in the right lung. These continue to subdivide into still smaller and smaller bronchi within the lungs until the decreasing cartilage disappears altogether, leaving only the air tubes, or bronchioles. Again, the bronchioles subdivide repeatedly until the branches reach into the ducts (alveolar ducts) leading into air sacs (alveolar sacs) whose walls have numerous, rounded projections called alveoli. The epithelial lining of the bronchioles is of the ciliated columnar type and provides air spaces for an easy exchange of gases between the surrounding blood capillaries and the air. In respiratory diseases, such as pneumonia, the air spaces may close because of inflamed alveoli which then produce materials that fill the spaces, creating dangerous consolidation of the lungs. Infection of the bronchi may cause bronchitis or other diseases such as bronchiectasis, marked by inflammation, chronic coughing, and congestion.

THE LUNGS

The lungs are cone-shaped, spongy, elastic, primary organs of respiration. They fill a substantial portion of the chest cavity. The part of the chest cavity between the lungs is the mediastinum; the part containing the heart is the pericardial division.

The left lung is narrower, longer, and smaller than the right and is divided into two lobes (upper and lower), whereas the right lung is divided into three lobes (upper, middle, and lower). The two primary bronchi enter each lung through the hilum, on the medial surface, along with the pulmonary blood vessels. Here the bronchi, arteries, veins, lymph vessels, nerves, and surrounding connective tissue form the root, from which the lung is suspended in the chest cavity. The pointed flap (apex) of the lung reaches to a level just above the first rib and sternum. The lower surface (base) rests on the diaphragm. Within each lung are millions of alveoli, along with the alveolar ducts, bronchioles, and bronchi. The pleura, a double-layered serous membrane, covers the lungs, the chest wall, and the diaphragm. A serum lubricates the two pleural layers so that the lungs move without friction during respiration.

DISORDERS OF THE RESPIRATORY SYSTEM

The entire respiratory tract is exposed to airborne infections. Upper respiratory infection (the common head cold) is apt to lead to paranasal sinus involvement (sinusitis), for the drainage openings are no longer at the bottom of the sinus cavities, as they used to be before man learned to walk upright. The infection may spread from tne nose to the ears (otitis) and to the mastoid via the Eustachian tubes. The tonsils may also become the seat of chronic infection, in which event they may have to be removed. Hoarseness is still another disorder arising from infection, in this instance involving the vocal cords (as in laryngitis). Persistent hoarseness may be due to chemical irritation (e.g., in excessive smoking) or to chronic catarrh, tuberculosis, syphilis, or tumors.

Serious disorders may affect the pleura. If air enters the pleural cavity as a result of injury or disease, the lungs will collapse, for they can no longer be inflated. (In some cases of lung disease, treatment may include the injection of air to collapse a lung for the purpose of resting it temporarily.) Infection of the pleura (pleurisy) gives rise to pain which is accentuated by deep breathing. Pleurisy may lead to the accumulation of fluid (pleural effusion), or an abscess may form (empyema). During the healing stage, the two layers of pleura may become adherent (pleural adhesions).

The lungs may become the seat of pneumonia, tuberculosis, dust accumulations (miner's phthisis), and tumors (benign or malignant). Great strides have been made however, in the treatment of lung infections by the administration of antibiotics. Improved methods of surgery have made it possible to remove tumors along with the portion of the lung involved or even the entire lung.

X—THE DIGESTIVE SYSTEM

The organs of the alimentary canal (the G.I. or gastrointestinal tract) and the accessory glands comprise the digestive system. The organs of the alimentary canal include the mouth, tongue, teeth, pharynx, esophagus, stomach, small intestine, and large intestine. The accessory glands include the salivary glands, the liver, the gallbladder, and the pancreas. The digestion of food is the chief function of these organs and glands. Digestion is the process of breaking complex foods down into soluble, absorbable materials, then absorbing or storing them and eliminating the waste products.

It will be helpful to review basic facts about the thoracic and abdominal cavities. They are separated by the diaphragm. The thoracic cavity is divided into the two pleural cavities (for the lungs) and the pericardial cavity for the heart. All these cavities have a lining of thin epithelium. The lining of the pleural cavities is called the pleura, that of the pericardial cavity is called pericardium, and that of the abdominal cavity is called the peritoneum.

The peritoneal covering connecting the liver and stomach is the lesser omentum. A double fold of peritoneum, the greater omentum, is attached to the duodenum and the stomach and extends downward, covering the intestines as if it were an apron. This double fold helps to localize any inflammation within the abdominal cavity; its fatty tissue also protects the organs and retains heat. Peritoneal lining completely surrounds and covers the stomach, jejunum, ileum, and transverse colon; it partially covers the liver, cecum, ascending colon and descending colon, rectum, and uterus; but the kidneys, urinary bladder, pancreas, duodenum, and blood vessels are located behind the peritoneum. A lubricating fluid of the peritoneum reduces friction between organs and between the linings and organs. In the posterior portion of the abdominal cavity, a double layer of peritoneum called the mesentery extends like a fan from the lumbar region; it supports the small intestine (duodenum, jejunum, and ileum) which is

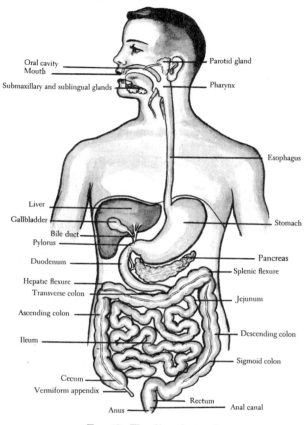

Oral cavity
Mouth
Submaxillary and sublingual glands
Parotid gland
Pharynx
Esophagus
Liver
Gallbladder
Bile duct
Pylorus
Duodenum
Hepatic flexure
Transverse colon
Ascending colon
Ileum
Cecum
Vermiform appendix
Anus
Stomach
Pancreas
Splenic flexure
Jejunum
Descending colon
Sigmoid colon
Rectum   Anal canal

FIG. 27. The digestive system.

attached to its outside edges, and it contains important blood
vessels and lymph vessels.

THE MOUTH

The mouth (buccal cavity) consists of a vestibule formed by
the lips, cheeks, gums, and teeth; and an oral cavity behind the
gums and teeth. The hard and soft palates form its roof; the
mylohyoid muscles and the tongue form its floor; and the cheeks
form its lateral walls. The hard palate is a bony structure forming a partition between the nasal and oral cavities. The soft palate is a fold of mucous membrane extending backward from the
hard palate, its edge (velum) hanging downward into the pharynx

and bearing a soft projection, the uvula. The soft palate moves upward to close the connection between the nasal and oral cavities during swallowing and speaking.

The tongue consists of muscular tissue covered with mucous membrane. The root of the tongue is attached to the floor of the mouth by means of a fold, the frenulum, in the midline of the under surface. ("Tongue-tied" speech may be caused by a frenulum that is too short.) On its surface the tongue has thread-like elevations called papillae, some of which contain important taste buds. Functions of the tongue are to move food around in the mouth, begin the swallowing action, aid in speech production, and provide equipment for taste sensations.

The body develops two sets of teeth. The temporary or baby set (deciduous teeth) consist of 20 teeth, 10 in each jaw as follows: 2 central incisors and 2 lateral incisors (shaped like a chisel); 2 canines (cuspids); and 4 molars (tricuspids). The permanent set of teeth (which generally replace the temporary set between the ages of 6 and 13 years) has, in addition, 4 premolars (bicuspids) that erupt at the ages of 10 to 12 years and 2 new molars (wisdom teeth) that erupt between the ages of 17 and 21 years. The part of each tooth above the gum is the crown. The next portion, or neck, is covered by gum. The bottom portion, the root, lies in a socket of the jaw bone. A vertical cut into a tooth exposes the following hard parts: the outside covering of enamel, the hardest substance in the body; dentine (forming the main part of the tooth) that has the structure of bone but is much harder; and cementum (also resembling bone) that covers the dentine in the root section and in part of the neck section. The soft parts of a tooth include the pulp in the interior, with its capillaries, lymph vessels, and nerve fibers; and a membrane (the periodontal membrane) that connects the cementum over the root with the alveolar bone and holds the root steady in the socket.

THE PHARYNX

The mechanisms of the pharynx automatically keep food from entering the windpipe. (The structure of the pharynx has been described in the discussion of the respiratory system.) In the process of swallowing, the tongue raises and propels a bolus of masticated food backward toward the pharynx; the pharyngeal muscles elevate the larynx and pharynx. The food passes over the epiglottis (now directed posteriorly as a shield), and the constrictor muscles of the pharynx then propel the food into the esophagus.

THE ESOPHAGUS

The esophagus is a highly muscular, collapsible tube about 10 inches long, extending from the neck through the thoracic cavity and diaphragm to the stomach area just below the diaphragm. The muscles of the esophagus propel the food through it and downward into the stomach by means of successive contractions (peristalsis). (Liquids pass down without requiring such propulsion.) As the food reaches the cardiac sphincter, the latter relaxes and the bolus proceeds into the stomach.

It may be noted that all muscle actions in the process of swallowing are reflex acts (except those of the tongue). Semisolid foods usually require about 6 seconds or longer to reach the stomach.

THE STOMACH

The stomach is a J-shaped organ located in the upper left portion of the abdominal cavity, its concave inside border (the lesser curvature) facing upward and to the right toward the duodenum, its convex outside border (the greater curvature) facing to the left and downward. About 85 per cent of its mass lies to the left of the midline of the body. Its four main parts are: (1) the portion with the opening (cardiac orifice) from the esophagus; (2) the fundus (or fornix), an expanded area above the opening to the esophagus and extending to the left; (3) the body; and (4) the pyloric section, with an expanded part (the pyloric antrum), a narrow canal (the pyloric canal), and an opening (pyloric orifice) into the duodenum. There are two sphincter muscles (bands of rounded fibers) which can relax to allow an opening through them and can also contract to close the opening. The orifice from the esophagus to the stomach is protected by the cardiac sphincter; the orifice from the pyloric canal into the duodenum is protected by the pyloric sphincter. The pyloric section varies in position, depending upon the individual's stature and body position, the amount of food distending the stomach, and the pressure from the contents of adjacent organs. The lower limit of the stomach in tall, thin persons may be almost as far down as the pubic bone. In short, stocky persons, the lower limit of this J-shaped organ may remain at a relatively high level, not much below the place where its pyloric end attaches to the duodenum. (See page 133.)

The four coats of the stomach are: (1) the mucosa, or innermost coat; (2) the submucosa, or connective tissue joining the mucosa and the muscular coat; (3) the muscular coat, consisting of three layers of tissue; and (4) the serosa, a thin, outer coat forming the greater omentum. When the stomach is empty, the mucosa curls into many folds, or rugae, which vanish when food distends the organ. In the mucosa are millions of tubular glands; some of the cells of these glands secrete pepsin, while others secrete hydrochloric acid. The gastric juices secreted by the glands also contain mucin, antianemia materials, and inorganic salts. The pepsin decomposes proteins into metaproteins, these into proteoses, and these into peptones. Pepsin cannot perform its function, however, without the aid of hydrochloric acid in the gastric juices. The muscular movements and the action of enzymes convert food into semiliquid chyme, an acid substance which causes the pyloric sphincter to relax, allowing the chyme to be propelled into the small intestine. It usually takes three to four hours for a meal to be digested in this way by action of the stomach juices.

THE SMALL INTESTINE

The small intestine is a coiled tube 22.5 feet long extending from the pylorus to the large intestine. Its three continuous sections are the duodenum (about 10 inches long) into which the bile duct and pancreatic ducts lead; the jejunum, about 9.5 feet long; and the ileum, about 12.5 feet long, extending from the jejunum to the large intestine. (The foregoing measurements applying to cadavers; the small intestine may be only about 5 or 6 feet long in living subjects.)

The main juices of the small intestine are bile, pancreatic juice, and intestinal secretions. The liver secretes about 500 cc. of bile daily. Bile is stored in the gallbladder; it then passes into the duodenum. It reduces the acidity of chyme, makes fatty acids more soluble, emulsifies fats, conveys waste products for excretion, aids the full utilization of proteins and carbohydrates, and stimulates the activity of the intestine. (Bile contains red-green pigments giving feces a brown color.) The liver and gallbladder also secrete cholesterol, which may cause the formation of gallstones. Pancreatic juice contains various enzymes for the digestion of proteins, starches, and fats. Intestinal juice (succus entericus) contains secretions of glands in the mucosa of the small intestine; water; salts; and various enzymes (and activators of enzymes) which convert proteoses, peptones, and peptids to amino acids and decompose nucleic acids. The various intestinal juices thus complete the processes of digestion.

THE LARGE INTESTINE

The large intestine is much wider than the small intestine and about 5 feet long. It begins as an arch to the right of the ileum, extends upward as the ascending colon above and in front of the small intestine, then crosses the entire abdomen horizontally to the left (transverse colon) and, finally, extends downward again as the descending colon on the left side of the abdomen, curving to the right at the bottom end as the S-shaped loop or sigmoid colon joining the rectum. Thus it nearly encircles the small intestine from the vermiform appendix at its lower left, upward and past the pancreas, thence downward to the anus. The large intestine has muscular bands (taeniae) along its entire length (2 bands in the sigmoid colon and rectum, 3 bands elsewhere); because the bands are shorter than the organ itself, characteristic, large, pocket-like folds (haustra) with fatty pouches on their surfaces are formed.

Note that the first and lowest portion of the large intestine is the cecum, about 3 inches long. Its closed lower end forms a blind pouch from which arises the appendix, a long, wormlike tube varying in length from 1 to 8 inches. Its upper end is continuous with the second portion (ascending colon) of the large intestine. The ileum, the terminal section of the small intestine, ends at an opening near the junction of the cecum with the ascending colon; here the ileocecal valve extends a short distance into the large intestine. This valve regulates the flow of digested food from the terminal ileum into the cecum and keeps food from flowing back into the ileum from the cecum. To repeat: the ascending colon makes a sharp left turn (at the right celic or hepatic flexure) to become the transverse colon; the latter extends to the left and turns downward (at the left celic or splenic flexure) to become the descending colon; the lowest right turn forms the sigmoid colon which continues as the rectum.

The rectum, about 5 inches long, consists of three dilated projections, one of which (the ampulla) connects with the anal canal (1.5 inches long). In the anal canal are sphincter muscles which compress the rectal wall and, working with the levator ani muscle, control the closure of the canal.

The main functions of the large intestine are to absorb water (so that the feces excreted are semisolid) and to excrete waste products, such as calcium, iron, magnesium, and phosphates. In addition, the bacteria in the large intestine cause fermentation of food, decomposing the carbohydrates into alcohol and acids, and acting on the proteins to produce amines, acids, and the gases that cause the typical odor of feces. The toxic amines either are eliminated or are purified by the liver; otherwise, the condition of autointoxication may result.

THE SALIVARY GLANDS

The salivary glands (parotid, submandibular, and sublingual glands) outside and the lingual, buccal, palatine, and labial glands inside the buccal cavity produce most of the 2 to 3 pints of saliva secreted daily.

Saliva is 98 per cent water, plus small amounts of mucin, mineral salts, enzymes, and organic compounds. The mucin binds food particles together into a bolus for swallowing and lubricates the buccal cavity The mineral salts are seen in tartar deposits on the teeth. The enzymes convert starches to maltose and maltose to dextrose. In general, saliva moistens the mucosa to aid swallowing (deglutition) and speech; dissolves foods sufficiently to facilitate mastication and to stimulate taste buds; to some extent cleanses and neutralizes the mouth; and helps to eliminate undesirable materials from the blood stream. Among common ailments is mumps, a virus disease affecting the parotid and other salivary glands.

THE LIVER AND GALLBLADDER

Below the diaphragm in the upper right area of the abdominal cavity is the liver, the largest gland of the body, about 10 inches wide and weighing about 3 or 4 pounds. It has four lobes: right, quadrate, caudate, and left—separated by fissures through one of which (the portal fissure between the quadrate and caudate lobes) pass the hepatic artery, portal vein, and common bile duct. A membrane (Glisson's capsule) extends around these structures and over the entire surface of the liver excepting an area adjoining the diaphragm. The common bile duct (formed by the common hepatic duct and the cystic duct) leads into the duodenum below the pyloric opening of the stomach.

The narrow neck of the gallbladder is continuous with the cystic duct. The larger portion of the pear-shaped gallbladder extends about 4 inches along the right lobe of the liver; its base projects past the lower end of the liver, rests on the transverse colon, and is directed downward and to the right.

As already mentioned, one of the main functions of the liver is the secretion of bile. (Other functions will be recalled: blood formation and manufacture of anti-clotting heparin, pro-clotting prothrombin, and fibrinogen; storage of proteins, fats, glycogen, minerals, and vitamins; detoxication of harmful substances; and the production of body heat.) The gallbladder concentrates and stores bile. Crystallized fat particles (particularly cholesterol) and other substances may accumulate in this organ or in the bile ducts and form gallstones. Passage of these concretions through the ducts may be extremely painful. If there is complete obstruction, the bile is absorbed into the blood, causing jaundice characterized by a yellowish coloring from bile pigments in the skin and membranes.

THE PANCREAS

Below the liver and stomach lies the pancreas, a tubular straw-colored gland with two main sections: a head, along the inner curve of the duodenum, and a narrower portion (consisting of a neck, body, and tail) extending horizontally, slightly upward and to the left (behind the stomach), reaching the spleen. The pancreas is about 6 or 7 inches long and weighs on the average about 3.5 ounces. It has two types of cells: (1) pancreatic duct cells that secrete pancreatic juice (which flows through ducts into the duodenum); and (2) ductless cells, called the islands of Langerhans, that secrete the insulin hormone which is given off into the blood. (The hormone secretin, secreted by the duodenum, flows into the blood stream to the pancreas, where it increases pancreatic secretion and concentrates the bicarbonates in the pancreatic juice, an important factor in the final processes of digestion.) Insulin is necessary for proper utilization of blood sugar. Reduced insulin production resulting from disease in the island cells causes diabetes mellitus. (Note the illustration and discussion of the pancreas, page 158.)

DIGESTION

Digestion is the entire process in the alimentary tract whereby foods are changed into simpler compounds. The first steps are mastication (to reduce the size of food particles and mix them with mucin and saliva) and deglutition (whereby each bolus of food is propelled from the mouth through the pharynx and the esophagus to the stomach). The next step is the action of the stomach in churning the food, mixing it with gastric juices and converting the food into chyme. (Branches of the vagus nerve, the 10th cranial nerve, exercise reflex control over gastric secretions; in cases of gastric ulcers, it is sometimes helpful to divide the nerve surgically in order to diminish the secretions. Among the chemicals stimulating the secretions are histamine, found in gastric juice; the hormone gastrin, produced by the pyloric mucosa; and caffeine.) Constricting followed by relaxing movements in the stomach (peristalsis) force the food in successive amounts into the duodenum.

It may take 3 or 4 hours to empty the stomach. Churning and peristalsis continue in the small intestine, mixing the food thoroughly with the digestive juices. The food remains in the small intestine several hours, and it is here that many of the digestive food products are further churned and then absorbed by the blood and lymph. Similar movements, but at a slower rate, continue in the large intestine. The food residues mixed with bacteria may remain in the lower colon and rectum for 24 hours or longer before peristalsis and abdominal muscle contractions result in evacuation.

It should be noted at this point that digested food proteins and carbohydrates are absorbed by the blood and thus carried via the portal vein to the liver, hepatic vein, inferior vena cava, heart, and throughout the body. Excess carbohydrate (glucose) is converted to glycogen and stored in the liver for future use. Fats are absorbed by lymph in the form of glycerol or in a water-soluble combination with bile.

METABOLISM

Metabolism refers to the ways in which the body uses absorbed foods. It burns them to get heat and energy for its activities (catabolism); it makes protoplasmic tissue from them (anabolism) for growth and repair and for the manufacture of secretions, such as hormones. Carbohydrates and fats provide most of the heat energy used by the body; proteins are converted into amino acids, which provide cells for new protoplasm and the repair of tissues and are synthesized into enzymes and hormones.

The term *basic metabolic rate* refers to the least amount of heat the body must produce in order to remain alive while at rest but awake during a twenty-four hour period. It indicates the amount of food needed for maintaining vital functions (e.g., circulation, respiration, digestion). This amount will vary with factors such as body size, age, and the condition of the endocrine glands which can increase or reduce the metabolic rate.

DISORDERS OF THE DIGESTIVE SYSTEM

Common dental ailments include tooth decay (caries) and gum infection (pyorrhea). Spreading of infection to the roots of teeth or around impacted teeth often causes absorption of poisons (toxins) into the blood and may produce symptoms of "rheumatism" or "neuralgia." Chronic infection of the tonsils is another type of "focal infection." Acute infection of the tonsils may lead to the formation of an abscess (quinsy). Since any focus of infection menaces vital organs, such foci are usually removed.

Abdominal structures are subject to crushing accidents or penetrating wounds; internal hemorrhage and the danger of infection of the internal lining (peritonitis) necessitate prompt remedial action. Emergencies may also arise from acute infections of the gallbladder (cholecystitis) and of the appendix (appendicitis), from perforation or bleeding of a peptic ulcer (gastric or duodenal), and from snaring of loops of intestine through narrow abdominal openings, as in rupture (strangulated hernia). Immediate operation is usually necessary in this group of acute emergencies.

Emotions have a direct influence on the functioning of intestinal organs. In many cases of peptic ulcer, colitis, and spasms of the intestinal tract, nervous tension is considered one of the basic causes. Nutrition is another potent factor. Dietetic indiscretions, such as overindulgence in spices or excessive use of roughage, may cause digestive disturbances. Irregular meals may lead to delay in the orderly onward propulsion of food (peristalsis) by action of the intestinal muscles. This delay often results in abdominal cramps and excessive gas accumulations in the right and left upper abdomen where the large intestine (colon) turns sharply at the right (hepatic) and left (splenic) colic flexures. "Gas pockets" in the latter position are likely to elevate the left dome of the diaphragm and thus exert pressure on the heart with consequent discomfort in the heart region. Finally, the excessive use of alcohol and the resulting disturbance of nutrition may cause destruction of liver cells, ending in cirrhosis of the liver.

XI—THE URINARY SYSTEM

Waste products are eliminated from the body through the skin, lungs, intestines, and urinary system. The kidneys contribute a large share of the work required to eliminate toxic substances and to maintain water balance, acid-base equilibrium of body fluids, and the proper amount of salts and other materials in the blood. These are the functions performed mainly by the kidneys and other organs of the urinary system as it manufactures and eliminates urine.

The urinary system consists of two kidneys, two ureters (excretory tubes), one urinary bladder (a bag for storage and expulsion of urine), and one urethra (a duct from the bladder to the outside of the body).

THE KIDNEYS

The kidneys, in the adult, measure about 4.5 inches long, 2 to 3 inches wide, and a little over 1 inch thick. They are slightly longer in men than in women. They are located on each side of the vertebral column, just behind the peritoneum of the abdominal wall, extending vertically from a level above the waistline upward to the level of the 12th rib. The right kidney is pressed down by the liver and is therefore somewhat lower than the left. (See illustrations, pages 131–132.)

The kidneys, resembling a pair of lima beans turned on the flat side, are embedded in fat which helps to support them. In the middle of each kidney surface is a concave indentation, the hilum, through which the blood vessels, lymph vessels, and nerves enter and from which the ureter emerges. Tough, white fibers form a capsule around the kidney. Connective sheets of tissue help to keep the kidneys in position. Since the kidneys touch the diaphragm, they necessarily move with it when air is drawn into the lungs.

A longitudinal cut in the kidney discloses its internal structure, consisting of the outer granular portion, or cortex, and the striated inner portion, or medulla. The medulla consists of cone-shaped

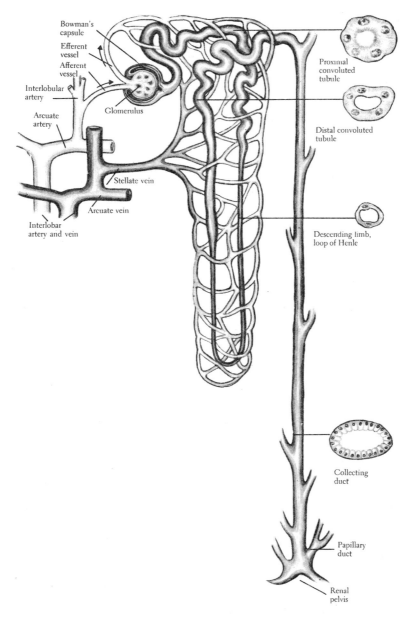

Bowman's
capsule

Efferent
vessel

Afferent
vessel

Interlobular
artery

Glomerulus

Arcuate
artery

Stellate vein

Arcuate vein

Interlobar
artery and vein

Proximal
convoluted
tubule

Distal convoluted
tubule

Descending limb,
loop of Henle

Collecting
duct

Papillary
duct

Renal
pelvis

FIG. 28. A nephron.

pyramids. Each pair of pyramids is separated by columns (the renal columns) extending from the cortex into the medulla as far as the inner opening (the renal sinus) near the hilum. In the central portion of the renal sinus is a cavity (the renal pelvis) which is the expanded end of the ureter and includes cup-shaped tissues (calyces) that enclose the ends (papillae) of the pyramids.

Microscopic examination shows each kidney to be composed of more than a million (perhaps as many as 4 million) units called nephrons. Each nephron consists of a renal corpuscle (corpuscle of Malpighi) and a tubule The corpuscle is a cluster of looped capillaries (a glomerulus) enclosed by the renal capsule (Bowman's capsule) ; it contains two convoluted parts (between which is a loop—the loop of Henle), one of which leads into a straight collecting duct. The straight collecting ducts give the medulla of the kidney its striated appearance; the other parts of the nephron are mainly in the cortex. The nephrons in the two kidneys have about 45 miles of tubules.

The kidneys produce urine by filtering the water and minerals out of the blood (carried along the afferent arteries of the renal artery to the looped capillaries of the corpuscles), while leaving the blood cells in the capillaries. The fluid thus taken out of the blood travels to the renal pelvis through the tubules. During this passage, 99 per cent of the fluid is reabsorbed into the blood surrounding the tubules, including some glucose, potassium, and calcium. Since urea, uric acid, and phosphates are not readily absorbed, they remain in the urine and are eliminated with it, as are non-absorbable substances, such as the sulfates.

About 1500 cc. of urine is excreted daily, the amount varying with the diet, water ingestion and loss, and the degree of physical activity of the individual. Nerve impulses stimulating the arteries and veins to the kidneys affect the secretion of urine. Hormones in the blood influence the reabsorbing action of the tubules and affect the amount of water. salts, and other substances excreted.

URETERS

The urine excreted by the kidneys passes through the ureters. The ureter is a duct 10 to 12 inches long, connecting the renal pelvis with the urinary bladder. (The right ureter connects to the right kidney, which is located lower down than the left kidney; therefore, the right ureter is shorter than the left.) Each ureter has three coats: a mucous inner layer, a middle muscular coat of two layers, and an outer layer of connective fibers. The alternating contracting and relaxing movements of the muscular coat squirt the urine downward and into the bladder. The ureter has only a narrow passageway throughout its length; if kidney stones develop in the kidney, the urine may carry some of the smaller concretions into a ureter expanding its walls and causing severe pain (renal colic).

THE BLADDER

The urinary bladder lies in the front portion of the pelvic cavity. In the male, it is in front of the rectum; in the female, it is in front of the vagina and uterus. When the bladder fills with urine, a membrane at each of the superior openings to the ureters prevents the urine from flowing back into the ureters. The bladder can retain about 1 pint of urine.

Branches of the internal iliac arteries (and, in women, of the vaginal and uterine arteries) carry blood to the bladder. Veins from the bladder empty into the internal iliac vein. Nerves of the autonomic system stimulate the muscles which act to retain or to expel urine. When the bladder is distended with urine, nerve fibers react to initiate urination (micturition).

THE URETHRA

In the male, the urethra is about 8 inches long and is continuous with the neck of the bladder; it carries both urine and semen. The first portion, about 1 inch long, is surrounded by the prostate gland; the second (membranous) portion is the shortest and narrowest, extending from the prostate to the bulb of the penis; and the third (spongy) portion, about 6.5 inches long, extends through the penis. In the female, the urethra serves only as an excretory duct. It is about 1.5 inches long, extending along the frontal surface of the vagina, with the external opening (urethral orifice) in the vestibule between the vaginal orifice and the clitoris.

URINE

The amount of urine formed averages about 3 pints daily. Urine is about 95 per cent water, the balance consisting of organic substances (including urea, uric acid, and hippuric acid) and inorganic substances (including sodium chloride, potassium chloride, sulfuric acid, phosphoric acid, ammonia, calcium, and magnesium). The acidity of urine rises markedly in diseases such as diabetes mellitus. Urinalysis may disclose the presence of substances which are not normal constituents of urine. Thus, sugar or acetone in the urine may indicate diabetes mellitus; albumin may indicate kidney disturbances or disease; blood, pus, or casts may indicate kidney injuries, urinary tract infections, or abnormal growths within the urinary system.

DISORDERS OF THE URINARY SYSTEM

The production of urine starts with filtration of water and water-soluble minerals through the glomeruli. The body has special anatomical arrangements which assure a maximum blood pressure in the glomerular capillaries. Thus, the afferent blood vessel carrying blood to the glomerulus is of a larger caliber than the outflow blood vessel (efferent vessel). A low blood pressure due to weak heart action will lead to an inadequate pumping out of excess water, causing an accumulation of fluid in the tissues (edema, "dropsy").

Since the kidneys must remove waste products from the blood stream, these organs are exposed to toxic materials and are readily subject to infection. Resulting damage to kidney cells is termed Bright's disease (nephritis). In acute forms of this disease, the production of urine may be suppressed (anuria). Renal arteriosclerosis, characterized by the destruction of arterioles, is an example of chronic forms of the disease. In both acute and chronic conditions, the destruction of nephrons may impair the purification of the blood and cause an accumulation of waste materials (urea), eventually producing the toxic condition of uremia.

Stones (calculi) are solid deposits derived from the urine. If these form in the kidneys, they are usually carried downward along one of the ureters. The narrowest portion of this tube is situated just above the entrance to the bladder, where the calculus may become impacted. The passage of these solid and often rough substances causes severe pain (renal colic). The calculus may finally be passed via the bladder and urethra; otherwise, it must be removed by operation.

Men in older age groups are in many cases subject to disorders of the prostate gland, which is apt to enlarge and thus compress the first portion of the urethra. If this condition seriously impedes the flow of urine, surgical relief (prostatectomy) may become necessary.

XII—THE REPRODUCTIVE SYSTEM

The reproductive organs of the male include the two testes, a duct system, accessory glands, and the penis. The reproductive organs of the female include the two ovaries, the two uterine tubes, the uterus, the vagina, the vulva (external genitalia), and the two breasts (mammary glands). Some of the structures of the female are homologous to those of the male.

MALE REPRODUCTIVE ORGANS

The following paragraphs describe the principal reproductive organs and functions of the male. In general, the male reproductive system functions to manufacture male sex cells, provide means of copulation, secrete seminal fluid, and convey spermatozoa to the reproductive organs of the female.

Testes

Each testis is oval in shape, about 2 inches long, 1 inch wide, less than 1 inch thick, with its rounded front border free; its superior posterior portion contains ducts connecting it with a thin tube (the epididymis) which curls back along its side and top surfaces. The two testes are enclosed within one skin-like sac, the scrotum, located outside the abdominal cavity. The outer layer of thick fibers covering the testis is called the tunica albuginea. Inside this layer each testis is subdivided by partitions (septae) into about 250 lobules. Each lobule contains 1 to 3 coiled tubules (seminiferous tubules) which join to form a straight tubule. The straight tubules lead to a center, the rete testes, where the ducts connect with the epididymis. The sperm cells and seminal fluids are produced in the seminiferous tubules and are stored in the epididymis temporarily. (For further details and illustration, see pages 163–164.) The interstitial cells in the testis produce male hormones, including testosterone, carried into the blood stream. These hormones are essential for the development of the secondary sex characteristics of the male

It is significant that in the embryo the testes move down from the abdominal cavity (near the kidneys) through the ventral wall of the abdomen to the scrotum. In this process they pass (along with the spermatic cord of ducts, blood vessels, and nerves) through a canal, the inguinal canal. This canal has an internal ring (internal opening) and a subcutaneous ring (external opening). (Since the external inguinal rings are larger in the male than they are in the female, a sac of fat or intestine can pass through them more easily, either indirectly, along with the spermatic cord, or directly into the ring though a weak part of the abdominal wall. For this reason, inguinal hernia is more common in men than in women.) Sperm cells do not develop properly in undescended testes because of the higher temperature within the body cavity. Unless one or both testes descend during birth, or can be moved down surgically, sterility results.

The Epididymis

The epididymis, draped halfway around the testis, has an upper head portion and a lower tail portion. The straight tubes leading from the testis become highly coiled and extend into a single, coiled duct, the ductus epididymis. This duct extends downward into the tail portion and joins an ascending duct, the ductus deferens, or vas deferens. It is the latter duct which extends upward inside the spermatic cord and through the inguinal canal, then crosses the pelvis, and continues over the top and posterior border of the bladder and past the ureter. As it passes the ureter, it turns downward sharply and becomes enlarged as an ampulla, or dilated sacculated portion. Here it is joined by the seminal vesicle (a membranous pouch) and continues downward with the duct of the latter to form the narrow ejaculatory duct. The ejaculatory duct extends through the prostate gland and urethra (the three portions of which have been described in the discussion of the urinary system)

Male Accessory Glands

The accessory reproductive glands of the male are the seminal vesicles, the prostate gland, and the bulbo-urethral glands. The two seminal vesicles, located above the prostate gland and behind the posterior border of the urinary bladder, produce a part of the seminal fluid. The prostate gland is a bilobed tubular gland below the bladder, at which point it surrounds the urethra. (Enlargement of the prostate causes compression of the urethra so that urine cannot readily pass through the tube. In severe cases, surgical removal of the gland becomes necessary.) The prostate gland actually consists of 30 to 50 alveolar glands with ducts leading into the urethra. Its alkaline secretion mixed in the semen seems to activate the sperm. The two small pea-shaped bulbo-urethral glands. (Cowper's glands) are located below the prostate gland on each side, just over the bulb of the penis, and secrete a mucuslike lubricating fluid.

The Penis

The penis is a vascular structure of erectile tissue about 4 to 6 inches long, containing arterioles and blood spaces. It consists of three parts: a root, a body, and an end portion, the glans penis. The root is the part attached to the underside of the pubic arch by the suspensory ligament and by a more superficial ligament (fundiform ligament) connecting with the membranous tissue of the abdomen. The body consists of three cylindrical masses of erectile tissue bound by tissue fibers and a skin covering. Two of these masses (the corpora cavernosa penis) extend side by side (separated by a septum) to form the upper portion; the third mass (corpus spongiosum penis, or corpus cavernosum urethrae) is the lower portion which encloses the urethra. The extreme end of this third cylindrical mass includes the conical bulge called the glans penis and a slit or opening—the external urethral orifice. The skin is folded over the glans penis as a foreskin or prepuce; circumcision removes the prepuce. Ejaculation from the penis emits from 200 million to 400 million sperm cells, which retain their fertilizing ability for about 24 hours thereafter.

FEMALE REPRODUCTIVE ORGANS

The following paragraphs describe the principal reproductive organs and functions of the female. (See the illustrations on pages 141–143.) These are concerned mainly with the manufacture of female sex cells, fertilization and embryonic development, menstruation, and pregnancy.

The Ovaries

The ovaries are two almond-shaped bodies about 1.5 inches long, 1 inch wide, located adjacent to the side walls of the pelvis. Three structures (the mesovarium or mesentery connecting to the broad ligament, the ovarian ligament to the uterus, and the suspensory ligament to the pelvic wall) hold each ovary in place. The outer layer (cortex) of each ovary contains germinal epithelial cells which grow inward and produce follicles numbering about 200,000 in the adult female. Each follicle contains an ovum, which increases in size as it matures until it occupies as much as a fourth of the entire ovary and protrudes from its surface (Graafian follicle). The ovary, too, expands, and at this stage the follicle may regress and disappear or it may thin out because of its internal fluid pressure so as to release the ovum which, with the fluid and surrounding cells (corona radiata or discus proligerus) flows gently into the pelvic cavity.

The discharge of an ovum in this manner (called ovulation) occurs 10 days after cessation of the menstrual flow; it occurs every 28 days during adult life until the menopause. The average female infant is born with about 400,000 primitive follicles, but only about 400 follicles mature and discharge ova during a lifetime. After discharging an ovum, the rest of the follicle changes into a yellow body (corpus luteum) which grows for 12 to 14 days and then degenerates if the ovum is not fertilized. But if the ovum is fertilized, the corpus luteum continues to grow during the first 5 or 6 months of pregnancy.

In addition to the development of ova, the ovarian follicles manufacture a hormone (estradiol) which stimulates growth of the uterine lining and produces the female secondary sex characteristics. The cells of the corpus luteum manufacture the hormone progesterone (the gestation hormone) required for the early development of the fertilized ovum and for other functions connected with uterine glands, ovulation, uterine contractions, and activation of mammary glands.

The Uterine Tubes (Oviducts)

The two uterine tubes (Fallopian or ovarian tubes) are about 4.5 inches long, extending between the folds of the broad ligament

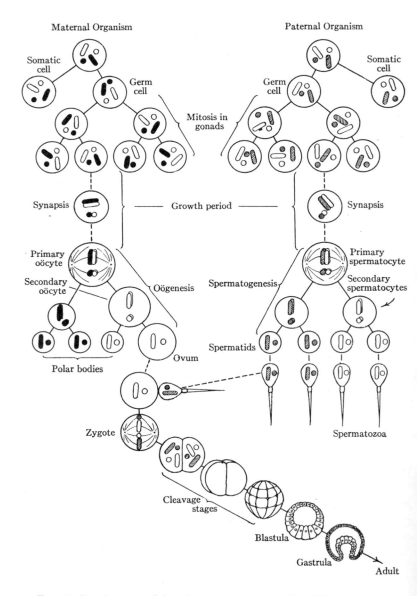

FIG. 29. Development of female and male germ cells. Diagram shows the continuity of chromosomes from the gametes which form two parents, through the germ cells in the gonads of these individuals, to the embryo which is their progeny. (From Gordon Alexander, *Biology,* College Outline Series.)

from the uterus upward to an area beyond the ovary. Each tube has three parts: (1) the narrow lower part or isthmus, attached to the uterus; (2) the wide and long ampulla, which extends over the ovary; and (3) a superior end portion, the infundibulum (with its fringed, branched processes or fimbriae) that surrounds the opening (ostium) into the pelvic cavity. Since the mucous lining joins the peritoneum, infections from the vagina and uterus may spread into the peritoneal cavity, causing inflammation (peritonitis).

A discharged ovum enters the uterine tube at its infundibulum, propelled by cilia on the contracting muscle fibers of the tube. Fertilization of the ovum occurs in this portion of the tube after the entrance of sperm from the uterus. The zygote (fertilized ovum resulting from impregnation by the spermatozoon and fusion of the two nuclei) divides into segments in the tube and normally reaches the uterus in about 8 days afterward. Inflammation of the uterine tube may impede passage of the zygote and result in tubal (ectopic) pregnancy.

The Uterus

The pear-shaped uterus, about 3 inches long, consists of a fundus, or body (the upper, expanded portion), a short constricted isthmus about 1 cm. long, and a lower neck, or cervix, about 2 cm. long, which extends into the upper vagina. The body cavity of the uterus is a small triangular area between the two thick sides. On each upper side a uterine tube enters the cavity. A narrow extension of the body cavity constitutes the cervical canal, and its opening into the vagina is called the external os. The front of the uterus is separated from the urinary bladder by the vesicouterine pouch, a space lined with peritoneum; the posterior portion is separated from the rectum by the recto-uterine pouch, another space which extends downward to the vagina. The uterus is supported in its position (its anterior surface resting on the top surface of the bladder and its cervix tapering slightly downward at an angle with the vagina) by cervical ligaments (the round ligament at the fundus, the broad ligament to the pelvis, and the uterosacral, or recto-uterine, ligament from the cervix to the sacrum). The body of the uterus can move with considerable freedom and can change to an abnormal (excessively vertical or excessively horizontal) position.

The uterus has several functions: (1) its inner layers, the endometrium or mucosa, are sloughed off and discharged in the menstrual flow (through the vagina) during the first five days of menstruation; (2) the fertilized ovum becomes a blastocyst (a mass of cells formed through cell division within 10 days after fertilization) which enters and implants itself in the endometrium, where it grows and develops; (3) uterine muscles contract to assist in the birth process of expelling the fetus; (4) uterine blood vessels provide nutriments for the embryo and remove waste products.

The Vagina

The vagina, a muscular, distensible tube, is about 3 inches long and extends from the cervix of the uterus to the external genitalia. At its superior end there is a groove, the fornix, which surrounds the projecting cervix. Its wall has a top mucous layer (mucosa) with numerous blood vessels; a muscular layer; and an elastic, fibrous layer. A posterior partition separates the vagina from the rectum; and an anterior partition separates the vagina from the bladder and urethra. Its main functions are to receive semen from the male during copulation, to discharge the menstrual flow, and to provide a canal for the passage of the fetus during childbirth. (See the illustration and discussion on page 143.)

The Vulva

The external genitalia, or vulva, include the two outer folds of skin (the labia majora), continuous with the mons veneris, a prominence of tissue covering the symphysis pubis; two smaller folds (the labia minora) located within the larger ones and extending 4 cm. backward from the clitoris; the clitoris, a small erectile organ at the junction of the smaller folds, which unite in front to form its covering, the foreskin or prepuce of the clitoris; the urinary meatus or orifice of the urethra, located between the vaginal orifice and the clitoris; and the vaginal orifice, on each side of which are the openings of the lubricating glands, the vestibular (Bartholin's) glands. The area between the genitalia and the anus is known as the obstetrical perineum; here an incision is sometimes made to minimize tearing during childbirth.

The Mammary Glands

The mammary glands, for the secretion of milk, are modified sweat glands enclosed within the convex breasts (mammae) located on the front surface of the thorax anterior to the pectoralis major muscle. The 15 to 20 lobes comprising each breast are separated by partitions (interlobular septa) of connective tissue. Within each lobule is an excretory duct. The ducts converge toward the central conical projection, the nipple. Around the nipple is a circular pigmented area, the areola, with many sebaceous glands and rudimentary milk glands. The mammary glands begin to secrete milk several days after delivery and keep providing milk as long as suckling is continued.

The Menstrual Cycle

From puberty (at the ages of 12 to 14) to the menopause (at the ages of 45 to 55) cells in the inner layer of the uterus die and are discharged through the vagina once each month of approximately 28 days. The menstrual cycle involves the following stages for the uterus: first 5 days—menstruation; next 2 days (start of postmenstrual period)—repairing the uterine layer of cells; next 8 days (of postmenstrual period)—growth and thickening (proliferation) of the uterine layer and glands; and next 13 days (premenstrual period)—winding and coiling of glands and secretion of glycogen, mucus, and fat. Failure to menstruate (at normal times during the interval from puberty to the menopause) may indicate pregnancy, or the presence of disease, or an endocrine disorder. Irregularities may also be caused by emotional disturbances.

The ovum is usually discharged about midway in the menstrual cycle (14 days after the start of menstruation), and the ovum can be fertilized only during the succeeding day or two; consequently, the week preceding and the week following the 5 days of menstruation are periods during which fertilization is unlikely.

The menopause usually begins in the years between 45 and 50; it is accompanied by a reduction in secretions of the reproductive glands; atrophy of the ovaries, uterus, and other sex organs; and physical and often psychological disturbances (hot flushes, headaches, sweating, dizzy spells, worry, fear, irritability). One cause of menopause difficulties may be lack of balance among the hormones in the body; administration of hormones may in some cases contribute to alleviation of the condition.

Pregnancy

In pregnancy, or gestation, menstruation ceases, the corpus luteum in the ovary becomes the corpus luteum of pregnancy and continues to secrete hormones essential for the development of the embryo.

Only one sperm cell is drawn into the protoplasm of the ovum. Then fertilization starts the process of cell division (segmentation) wherein a mass of cells (the morula) develops and moves through the uterine tube into the uterus. A cavity develops in the cell mass and enlarges into a layer of cells (the trophoblast), out of which an inner mass of cells projects in which the embryo grows as a blastocyst. The inner mass of cells soon differentiates into two layers—the upper, ectoderm layer and the lower, endoderm layer. Two cavities (the amniotic cavity and the yolk sac) appear in the mass of cells. Then a third layer of cells, the mesoderm, forms (in conjunction with the trophoblast) an important membrane, the chorion. Suspended from the chorion is the embryonic disc, consisting of three primary germ layers. All organs of the embryo develop from these three germ layers: from the ectoderm derive the nervous system and sense organs, epidermis, brain and spinal cord, hypophysis cerebri, anus, etc.; from the mesoderm derive the skeletal, muscular, circulatory, excretory, and reproductive systems, muscular and connective tissue, heart, blood vessels and organs, lymph vessels and organs, kidneys, ureters, testes, ovaries, uterine tubes, serous membranes, teeth, etc.; from the endoderm layer derive the respiratory and digestive systems, linings of the alimentary canal, pharynx, thyroid, liver, pancreas, gallbladder, larynx, trachea, lungs, urinary bladder, female urethra, prostate gland, and part of the male urethra.

The period of the embryo is about 50 days (to the end of the 2nd month), during which the body straightens, the main parts of the neck and face develop, a tail disappears after the sixth week, the genital organs begin to form, and bone, nerves, muscles, and sense organs develop. The period of the fetus is about 7 months, during which the head becomes proportionately smaller (because the rest of the body grows at a faster rate), sex organs are differentiated, hair appears, sense organs become well formed, and (in the 8th month) testes descend into the scrotum. The fetus in the 10th lunar month (at the age of 280 days) weighs about 7 pounds, with plump limbs, and is at full term. (See illustrations on pages 142–143.)

TWINS

Fraternal (diovular) twins develop from two separate ova and may be of the same or of opposite sex. They generally form separate membranes, with little or no fusion.

Identical (monovular) twins develop from a single, fertilized ovum which divides into two cell masses that grow as complete individuals. This division may occur within the original blastocyst, or it may occur later as the single mass of cells subdivide into two differentiated, analogous embryonic axes. There may be partial fusion, with separation possible after birth, or there may be extensive fusion of tissue and bone, resulting in "Siamese twins." Anomalies include babies with two heads or other duplicated body parts.

FETAL ABNORMALITIES

A great variety of abnormalities may occur; the science of teratology investigates their nature and etiology. Anomalies may be inherited or acquired. They may be structural or functional. Among the structural anomalies are missing fingers, arm, ear or other body parts; excessive development or duplication of parts; persistence of structures which should disappear (e.g., a tail); abnormal splitting of parts (e.g., cleft ureter) or failure to split (e.g., doubled digit); failure to fuse (e.g., cleft palate); excessive fusion (e.g., a horse-shoe kidney); failure of openings to close; excessive narrowing of an opening; abnormal misplacement or shifting of parts. Chemical, hormonal, or vitamin deficiencies, radioactive substances, and disease organisms may cause fetal abnormalities. German measles, for instance, if contracted by the mother early in her pregnancy, may cause deaf mutism and circulatory disorders in the fetus. The mechanisms of inherited abnormalities are unknown, although some of the abnormalities have been produced in experimental animals by exposure to radioactivity that affects the germ cells.

CHILDBIRTH

The terms labor and parturition refer to the expulsion of the fetus, a process which normally occurs in three stages.

In the first stage of labor, uterine contractions press the amniotic sac into the cervix, expanding it so that the head of the fetus is able, within a few hours, to move into the cervical canal, which is lubricated by fluid from the ruptured amnion.

In the second stage of labor, uterine contractions become more frequent and painful. At this stage, abdominal muscles aid the uterus in propelling the fetus through the vagina. The action of the uterus is involuntary, that of the abdominal muscles, voluntary. The delivery of the child is followed at once by ligation and then severance of the umbilical cord. This second stage of labor generally takes several hours. As the uterus continues its contractions, the remainder of the amniotic fluid is expelled.

In the third stage of labor, which may occur either within a few moments after delivery or after the lapse of several hours, the placenta (afterbirth) is expelled. Contractions of the uterus stop bleeding. Suckling maintains these contractions and also has psychological advantages for both mother and child. In addition, breast feedings transfer immune substances.

GROWTH OF THE INDIVIDUAL

Steen and Montagu divide the lifetime of the individual into the following periods:

1. Neonatal period, or period of the new-born, from birth to the end of the first month after birth. Feeding reflexes develop rapidly, although many responses appear to be generalized in nature, involving several body structures simultaneously. The neonate learns to hold the chin up.

2. Infancy, from the beginning of the second month to the beginning of the second year or 15 months. The infant learns to sit with help (4 months) and without help (7 months); to stand with help (8 months) and without help (14 months); to creep (10 months); and to walk unaided (15 months). Weight increases 200 per cent.

3. Childhood, subdivided into early childhood (ages 1 to 6 years), middle childhood (ages 6 to 10 years), and late childhood

(prepubertal period, ages 10 to 14 or 15 years). Growth is rapid during the first three or four years, slower thereafter until the twelfth year, and rapid again up to the eighteenth year. The brain, spinal cord, and many head dimensions increase rapidly in the first six years, then slowly for two or three years, and little thereafter. The lymphatic organs grow rapidly up to twelve years, not at all after that, whereas the sex organs and secondary sex characteristics develop rapidly beginning about the twelfth or thirteenth year.

4. Puberty begins in females with menstruation at age fourteen, in males during the fifteenth year. (In some cases, puberty may occur as early as age nine, in other cases as late as age twenty or above.)

5. Adolescence, from puberty to twenty-one years for women, twenty-four for men.

6. Maturity, from the end of the adolescent period to ages fifty-five or sixty.

7. Terminal age, the period after sixty, sometimes characterized in the later stages by a degree of enfeeblement.

DISORDERS OF THE REPRODUCTIVE SYSTEM

Sterility is often due to interference with the normal progress of sperm cells or ova. For example, scar formation after an infection may block tubules in the epididymis in the male. In the female, the opening (ostium) of a uterine tube may be closed by pelvic inflammation (pelvic peritonitis) or by infection of the uterine tubes (salpingitis).

After the ovum is fertilized in the uterine tube, its progress into the uterus may be impeded by abnormalities, such as inflammation or scarring. Implantation of the ovum in the uterine tube (tubal or ectopic pregnancy) may ensue. The clinical evolution in such cases starts with the appearance of the usual signs of pregnancy. But two or three months thereafter, abdominal pains may be experienced or the first warning may be a massive hemorrhage into the tube. In either event, the affected tube must be excised. If the remaining tube is unimpaired, subsequent normal pregnancies are possible.

In the management of pregnancy and labor, the basic guides are anatomical measurements, such as the diameters of the pelvis. The obstetrician determines the size and shape of the pelvis and the dimensions and position of the fetus. Difficulty may be caused by abnormal curvatures of the spinal column (see Chapter IV). If the forward curve of the lumbar spine becomes exaggerated (lordosis) or if the lower part of the spinal column deviates in other directions, passage of the fetus through the pelvis during labor may be delayed or even impossible. In such cases, delivery by Cesarian section may become necessary. This operation consists of opening the uterus through an abdominal incision.

ATLAS

OF

HUMAN ANATOMY

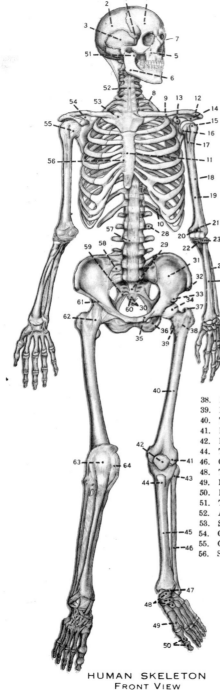

HUMAN SKELETON
FRONT VIEW

BONES, JOINTS AND LIGAMEN[

1. Frontal (*Os frontale*)
2. Parietal (*Os parietale*)
3. Temporal (*Os temporale*)
4. Sphenoid (*Os sphenoidale*)
5. Maxilla (*Maxilla*) 6. Mandible (*Mandibul*
7. Nasal (*Os nasale*)
8. First rib (*Costa I*)
9. Clavicle (*Clavicula*)
10. Twelfth rib (*Costa XII*)
11. Body of sternum (*Corpus sterni*
12. Acromion (*Acromion*)
13. Coracoid process (*Processus Coracoideus*)
14. Glenoid cavity (*Cavitas glenoidalis*)
15. Greater tubercle (*Tuberculum majus*)
16. Lesser tubercle (*Tuberculum minus*)
17. Bicipital groove (*Sulcus intertubercularis*)
18. Deltoid tuberosity (*Tuberositas deltoidea*)
19. Humerus (*Humerus*)
20. Coronoid fossa (*Fossa coronoidea*)
21. Radial fossa (*Fossa radialis*)
22. Coronoid process (*Processus coronoideus*)
23. Head of radius (*Caput radii*)
24. Ulna (*Ulna*) 25. Radius
26. **Carpal bones (*Ossa carpalia*)**
27. **Metacarpal bones (*Ossa metacarpalia*)**
28. Transv. process (*Processus transversus*)
29. Sacrum (*Os sacrum*) 30. Coccyx (*Os coccy*
31. Ilium (*Os ilium*)
32. Anterior superior iliac spine (*Spina ilia anterior superior*)
33. Anterior inferior iliac spine (*Spina ilia anterior inferior*)
34. Head of Femur (*Caput femoris*)
35. Pubic (*Os pubis*)
36. Superior branch of ischium (*Ramus superior ossis ischii*)
37. Great trochanter (*Trochanter major*)
38. Intertrochanteric line (*Linea intertrochanterica*)
39. Lesser trochanter (*Trochanter minor*)
40. Thigh bone (*Femur*)
41. Lateral condyle (*Condylus femoris lateralis*)
42. Knee cap (*Patella*) 43. Head of fibula (*Caput fibula*
44. Tuberosity (*Tuberositas tibiae*) 45. Shin bone (*Tib*
46. Calf bone (*Fibula*) 47. Ankle bone (*Malleolus late*
48. Tarsal bones (*Ossa tarsi*)
49. Metatarsal bones (*Ossa metatarsalia*)
50. Phalanges (*Phalanges*)
51. Temporo-mandibular ligament (*L. temporomandibu*
52. Anterior longitudinal lig. (*L. longitudinale anteriu*
53. Sternoclavicular joint (*Articulatio sternoclavicular*
54. Coracoclavicular ligament (*L. coracoclaviculare*)
55. Capsule of shoulder joint (*Capsula articularis hume*
56. Sterno-costal joint (*Articulatio sternocostalis*)
57. Intervertebral fibrocartilage (*Fibrocartilago intervertebralis*)
58. Sacro-iliac joint (*Articulatio sacroiliaca*)
59. Ligaments of sacrum and ischium (*L. Sacrospinosum et L. sacrotuberosum*)
60. Anterior sacro-coccygeal ligament (*L. sacrococcygeum anterius*)
61. Inguinal (Poupart's) ligament. (*L. inguinale*)
62. Iliofemoral ligament (*L. iliofemorale*)
63. Tendon of quadriceps muscle (*Tendo musculi quadricipitis*)
64. Capsule of knee-joint (*Capsula articulationis genu*)

Occipital (*Os occipitale*)
External occipital protuberance (*Protuberantia occipitalis externa*)
Sphenoid (*Os sphenoidale*)
Arch of zygoma (*Arcus zygomaticus*)
Seventh cervical vertebra (*Vertebra prominens cervicalis VII*)
First thoracic vertebra (*Vertebra thoracalis I*)
Twelfth rib (*Costa XII*)
First lumbar vertebra (*Vertebra lumbalis I*)
Sacrum (*Os sacrum*)   10. Coccyx (*Os coccygis*)
Shoulder blade (*Scapula*)
Head of humerus (*Caput humeri*)
Lateral epicondyle (*Epicondylus lateralis*)
Point of elbow (*Olecranon*)
Medial epicondyle (*Epicondylus medialis*)
Head of radius (*Capitulum radii*)
Tuberosity of radius (*Tuberositas radii*)
Base of radius (*Basis radii*)
Head of ulna (*Capitulum ulnae*)
Bones of the wrist (*Ossa carpalia*)
Bones of the hand (*Ossa metacarpalia*)
Hip bone (*Os coxae*)
Spine of ischium (*Spina ischiadica*)
Obturator foramen (*Foramen obturatorium*)
Tuberosity of ischium (*Tuber ischiadicum*)
Head of femur (*Caput femoris*)
Great trochanter (*Trochanter major*)
Intertrochanteric line (*Linea intertrochanterica*)
Lesser trochanter (*Trochanter minor*)
Rough line (*Linea aspera*)
Lateral condyle of femur (*Condylus lateralis femoris*)
Medial condyle of femur (*Condylus medialis femoris*)
Lateral condyle (*Condylus lateralis tibiae*)
Medial condyle (*Condylus medialis tibiae*)
Popliteal line (*Linea poplitea*)
Medial ankle bone (*Malleolus medialis*)
Ankle (*Talus*)   38. Heel (*Os calcaneum*)
Cuboid (*Os cuboideum*)
Metatarsal bones (*Ossa metatarsalia*)
Phalanges of the toes (*Phalanges*)
Ligament of the nape (*L. nuchae*)
Vertebral joint capsule (*Capsula articularis vertebrarum*)
Yellow ligament (*L. flavum*)
Supraspinous ligament (*L. supraspinale*)
Capsule of shoulder joint (*Capsula articularis humeri*)
Capsule of elbow joint (*Capsula articularis cubiti*)
Interosseous memb. (*Membrana interossea antebrachii*)
Wrist joint (*Articulatio radiocarpalis*)
Ilio-lumbar ligament (*L. iliolumbale*)
Interosseous sacro-iliac ligament (*L. sacroiliacum interosseum*)
Long posterior sacro-iliac ligament (*L. sacroiliacum posterius longum*)
Pubic symphysis (*Symphysis ossis pubis*)
Capsule of hip joint (*Capsula articularis coxae*)
Medial head of gastrocnemius (*Caput mediale M. gastrocnemii*)
Lateral head of gastrocnemius (*Caput laterale M. gastrocnemii*)
Oblique popliteal ligament (*L. popliteum obliquum*)
Tendon of semimembranosus (*T. M. semimembranosi*)
Collateral fibular ligament (*L. collaterale fibulare*)
Tibio-fibular artic. (*Articulatio tibiofibularis*)
Interosseous membr. (*Membrana interossea cruris*)
Posterior ligament of lateral ankle (*L. posterius malleoli lateralis*)

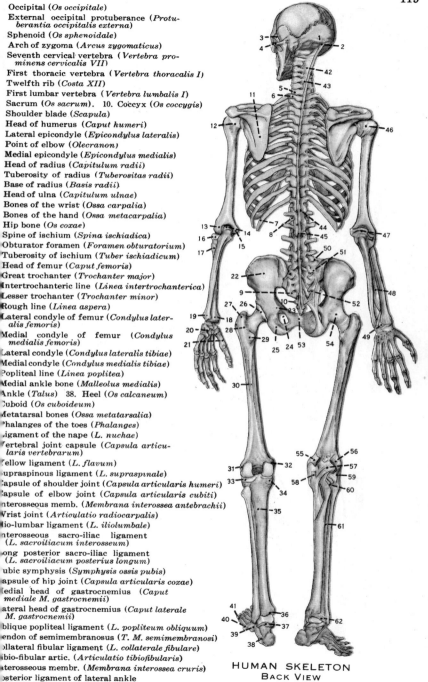

HUMAN SKELETON
BACK VIEW

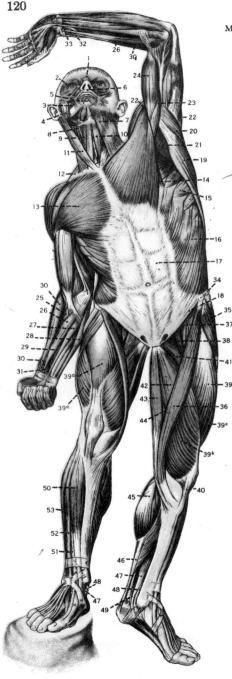

MUSCLES, TENDONS AND LIGAME[NTS]

1. Frontal (*M. frontalis*)
2. Orbicular of eye (*M. orbicularis oculi*)
3. Cheek (*M. buccinator*) 4. Masseter (*M. m[asseter]*)
5. Quadrate muscle of lower lip (*M. quadratus labii inferioris*)
6. Orbicular of mouth (*M. orbicularis oris*)
7. Flat (*M. platysma*)
8. Thyreohyoid (*M. thyreohyoideus*)
9. Omohyoid (*M. Omohyoideus*)
10. Sternohyoid (*M. sternohyoideus*)
11. Sternocleido-mastoid (*M. sternocleido-mastoideus*)
12. Trapezius (*M. trapezius*)
13. Greater pectoral (*M. pectoralis major*)
14. Smaller pectoral (*M. pectoralis minor*)
15. Serratus magnus (*M. serratus anterior*)
16. External oblique (*M. obliquus externus abdominis* [abdominis]
17. Sheath of rectus (*Vagina m. recti*[)]
18. Inguinal (Poupart's) lig. (*L. inguinale*)
19. Broadest muscle of back (*M. latissimus do[rsi]*)
20. Larger round (*M. teres major*)
21. Subscapular (*M. subscapularis*)
22. Deltoid (*M. deltoideus*)
23. Coraco-brachial (*M. coracobrachialis*)
24. Biceps (*M. biceps*)
25. Round pronator (*M. pronator teres*)
26. Radial flexor (*M. flexor carpi radialis*)
27. Long palmar (*M. palmaris longus*)
28. Ulnar flexor (*M. flexor carpi ulnaris*)
29. Superficial flexor of fingers (*M. flexor digitorum sublimis*)
30. Brachio-radial (*M. brachioradialis*)
31. Quadrate pronator (*M. pronator quadratus*)
32. Long abductor of thumb (*M. abductor pollicis longus*)
33. Deep flexor of fingers (*M. flexor digitorum profundus*)
34. Anterior superior iliac spine (*Spina iliaca anterior superior*)
35. Tensor of broad fascia (*M. tensor fasciae latae*)
36. Tailor (*M. sartorius*) 37. Iliac (*M. iliacus*[)]
38. Greater psoas (*M. psoas major*)
39. Four-headed thigh (*M. quadriceps femor[is]*)
39a. Straight head (*M. rectus femoris*)
39b. Middle great (*M. vastus medialis*)
39c. Lateral great (*M. vastus lateralis*)
40. Tendon of quadriceps (*Tendo M. quadricipitis femoris*)
41. Pectineus (*M. pectineus*)
42. Long adductor (*M. adductor longus*)
43. Slender (*M. gracilis*)
44. Great adductor (*M. adductor magnus*)
45. Gastrocnemius (*M. gastrocnemius*)
46. Achilles' tendon (*Tendo calcaneus*)
47. Long flexor of toes (*M. flexor digitorum longus*)
48. Posterior tibial (*M. tibialis posterior*)
49. Long flexor of toe (*M. flexor hallucis long[us]*)
50. Anterior tibial (*M. tibialis anterior*)
51. Long extensor of great toe (*M. extensor hallucis longus*)
52. Long extensor of toes (*M. extensor digitorum longus*)
53. Long peroneal ((*M. peronueus longus*)

MUSCLES—FRONT VIEW

MUSCLES, TENDONS AND LIGAMENTS

Occipital (*M. occipitalis*)
Semispinal (*M. semispinalis capitis*)
Splenius (*M. splenius capitis*)
Sternocleido-mastoid
  (*M. sternocleido-mastoideus*)
Trapezius (*M. trapezius*)
Broadest of back (*M. latissimus dorsi*)
Internal oblique
  (*M. obliquus internus abdominis*)
External oblique
  (*M. obliquus externus abdominis*)
Larger rhomboides (*M. rhomboideus major*)
Infraspinous (*M. infraspinalis*)
Smaller round (*M. teres minor*)
Larger round (*M. teres major*)
Spine of scapula (*Spina scapulae*)
Deltoid (*M. deltoideus*) 15. Triceps (*M. triceps*)
Brachial (*M. brachialis*) 17. Biceps (*M. biceps*)
Brachioradial (*M. brachioradialis*)
Long radial extensor of wrist
  (*M. extensor carpi radialis longus*)
Short radial extensor of wrist
  (*M. extensor carpi radialis brevis*)
Common extensor of fingers
  (*M. extensor digitorum communis*)
Long adductor of thumb
  (*M. adductor pollicis longus*)
Short extensor of thumb
  (*M. extensor pollicis brevis*)
Ulnar extensor of wrist
  (*M. extensor carpi ulnaris*)
Extensor of fifth finger
  (*M. extensor digiti quinti proprius*)
Dorsal ligament of wrist (*L. carpi dorsale*)
Abductor of fifth finger
  (*M. abductor digiti quinti*)
Round pronator (*M. pronator teres*)
Radial flexor (*M. flexor carpi radialis*)
Ulnar flexor (*M. flexor carpi ulnaris*)
Middle gluteal (*M. glutaeus medius*)
Greatest gluteal (*M. glutaeus maximus*)
Tensor of broad fasciae
  (*M. tensor fasciae latae*)
Great trochanter (*Trochanter major*)
Lateral great (*M. vastus lateralis*)
Biceps (*M. biceps femoris*)
Semitendinous (*M. semitendinosus*)
Semimembranous (*M. semimembranosus*)
Slender (*M. gracilis*)
Great adductor (*M. adductor magnus*)
Gastrocnemius (*M. gastrocnemius*)
Soleus (*M. soleus*)
Long peroneal (*M. peronaeus longus*)
Short peroneal (*M. peronaeus brevis*)
Long entensor of toes
  (*M. extensor digitorum longus*)
Third peroneal (*M. peronaeus tertius*)
Long flexor of great toe (*M. flexor hallucis longus*)
Achilles' tendon (*Tendo calcaneus*)
Anterior tibial (*M. tibialis anterior*)
Transverse ligament (*L. transversum cruris*)
Cruciate ligament (*L. cruciatum cruris*)
Heel bone (*Os calcaneus*)
Long flexor of toes
  (*M. flexor digitorum longus*)
Tendon of posterior tibial
  (*Tendo M. tibialis posterioris*)

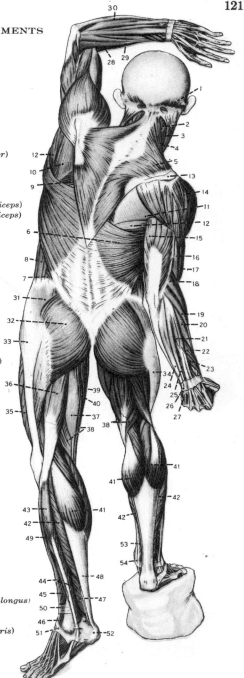

MUSCLES · BACK VIEW

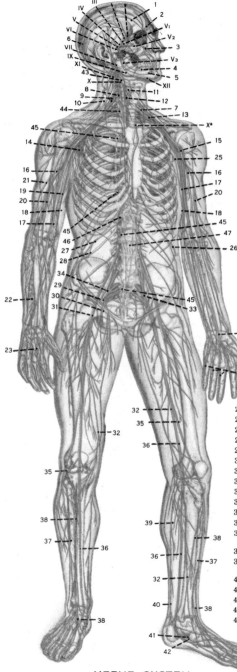

NERVE SYSTEM

NAMES OF NERVES

I. Olfactory (*N. olfactorius*)
II. Optic (*N. opticus*)
III. Oculomotor (*N. oculomotorius*)
IV. Trochlear (*N. trochlearis*)
V. Trigeminal (*N. trigeminus*)
V₁. *Ophthalmicus*, V₂. *Maxillaris*, V₃. *Mand*
VI. Abducent (*N. abducens*) VII. Facial (*N.*
IX. Glossopharyngeal (*N. glossopharyngeus*)
X. Right vagus (*N. vagus dexter*)
Xa. Left vagus (*N. vagus sinister*)
XI. Accessory (*N. accessorius*)
XII. Hypoglossal (*N. hypoglossus*)
   1. Supraorbital (*N. supraorbitalis*)
   2. Frontal (*N. frontalis*)
   3. Infraorbital (*N. infraorbitalis*)
   4. Lingual (*N. lingualis*) 5. Mental (*N. me*
   6. Occipital (*N. occipitalis major*)
   7. Left phrenic (*N. phrenicus sinister*)
   8. Right phrenic (*N. phrenicus dexter*)
   9. Supraclavicular (*Nn. supraclaviculares*)
   10. Dorsal of scapula (*N. dorsalis scapulae*)
   11. Superior laryngeal (*N. laryngeus super*
   12. Loop of hypoglossal (*N. ansa hypoglossi*
   13. Brachial plexus (*N. plexus brachialis*)
   14. Subscapular (*N. subscapularis*)
   15. Axillary (*N. axillaris*)
   16. Musculocutaneous (*N. musculocutaneus*
   17. Median (*N. medianus*) 18. Ulnar (*N. ul*
   19. Middle cutaneous
       (*N. cutaneus antibrachii medialis*)
   20. Radial (*N. radialis*)
       21. Posterior cutaneous
           (*N. cutaneus brachii posterior*)
       22. Dorsal interosseous
           (*N. interosseus dorsalis*)
       23. Anastomatic branch of ulnar
           (*N. ramus anastomaticus ulnaris*
       24. Proper volar digital
           (*Nn. digitales volares proprii*)
25. Intercostobrachial (*N. intercostobrachialis*)
26. Twelfth intercostal.(*N. intercostalis XII*)
27. Iliohypogastric (*N. iliohypogastricus*)
28. Ilioinguinal (*N. ilioinguinalis*)
29. External spermatic (*N. spermaticus externu*
30. Lumboinguinal (*N. lumboinguinalis*)
31. Femoral (*N. femoralis*)
32. Saphenous (*N. saphenus*)
33. Sacral plexus (*plexus sacralis*)
34. Superior gluteal (*N. glutaeus superior*)
35. Common peroneal (*N. peronaeus communis*)
36. Tibial (*N. tibialis*)
37. Superficial peroneal
    (*N. peronaeus superficialis*)
38. Deep peroneal (*N. peronaeus profundus*)
39. Medial cutaneous
    (*N. cutaneus surae medialis*)
40. Calf (*N. suralis*)
41. Medial plantar (*N. plantaris medialis*)
42. Lateral plantar (*N. plantaris lateralis*)
43. Superior cervical ganglion (*Ggl. cervicale su*
44. Inferior cervical ganglion (*Ggl. cervicale inj*
    45. Sympathetic trunk
        (*Truncus sympathicus*)
    46. Coeliac ganglion (*Ggl. coeliacum*)
    47. Inferior mesenteric ganglion
        (*Ggl. mesentericum inferius*)

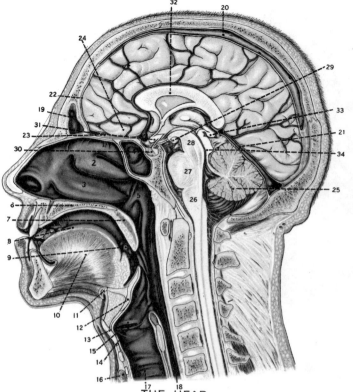

THE HEAD
MEDIAN SECTION

NAMES OF PARTS

1. Superior turbinated bone (*Concha nasalis superior*)
2. Middle turbinated bone (*Concha nasalis media*)
3. Inferior turbinated bone (*Concha nasalis inferior*)
4. Sphenoidal sinus (*Sinus sphenoidalis*)
5. Tubal protuberance (*Torus tubarius*)
6. Hard palate (*Palatum durum*)
7. Soft palate (*Palatum molle*)
8. Back of tongue (*Dorsum linguae*)
9. Tonsil (*Tonsilla palatina*)
10. Genioglossal muscle (*M. genioglossus*)
11. Hyoid bone (*Os hyoideum*)
12. Epiglottis (*Epiglottis*)
13. Thyroid cartilage (*Cartilago thyreoidea*)
14. Vocal fold (*Plica vocalis*)
15. Ventricular fold (*Plica ventricularis*)
16. Thyroid gland (*Glandula thyreoidea*)
17. Windpipe (*Trachea*)
18. Gullet (*Oesophagus*)
19. Frontal sinus (*Sinus frontalis*)
20. Superior sagittal sinus (*Sinus sagittalis superior*)
21. Straight sinus (*Sinus rectus*)
22. Dura mater (*Dura mater*)
23. Olfactory bulb (*Bulbus olfactorius*)
24. Frontal lobe (*Lobus frontalis superior*)
25. Worm of cerebellum (*Vermis cerebelli*)
26. Oblong medulla (*Medulla oblongata*)
27. Pons (*Pons*)
28. Leg of cerebrum (*Crus cerebri*)
29. Mamillary body (*Corpus mamillare*)
30. Pituitary body (*Hypophysis*)
31. Optic chiasma (*Chiasma nervi optici*)
32. Great commissure (*Corpus callosum*)
33. Pineal body (*Corpus pineale*)
34. Quadrigeminal bodies (*Corpora quadrigemina*)

The above illustrates beautifully how an infection in the nose may extend to the frontal sinus (19), sphenoidal sinus (4), middle ear (5), and lungs (17).

124

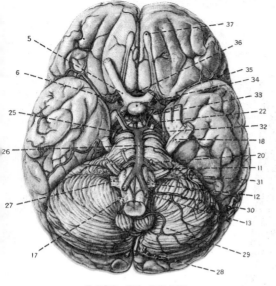

BASE OF BRAIN

NAMES OF PARTS

1. Frontal bone (*Os frontale*)
2. Ethmoid crest (*Crista galli*)
3. Dura mater (*Dura mater*)
4. Sphenoid bone (*Os sphenoidale*)
5. Optic nerve (*N. opticus*)
6. Internal carotid (*A. carotis intern*
7. Trigeminal nerve, ophthalmic part (*N. trigeminus, pars ophthalmic*
8. Trigeminal, maxillary part (*N. maxillaris*)
9. Cavernous venous plexus (*Plexus cavernosum venarum*)
10. Superior petrosal sinus (*Sinus petrosus superior*)
11. Stato-acoustic, facial, and interm* ate nerves and labyrinthine artery *stato-acusticus, N. facialis et intermedius et A. labyrinthi*)
12. Hypoglossal nerve (*N. hypoglossus*)
13. Vertebral artery (*A. vertebralis*)
14. Inferior cerebral vein (*V. cerebri inferior*)
15. Lateral sinus (*Sinus transversus*)
16. Straight sinus (*Sinus rectus*)
17. Spinal accessory nerve (*N. accessorius*)
18. Trigeminal nerve (*N. trigeminus*)
19. Middle meningeal artery and veins (*A. et Vv. meningeales mediales*
20. Abducent nerve (*N. abducens*)
21. Trigeminal, mandibular part (*N. mandibularis*)
22. Oculomotor nerve (*N. oculomotor*
23. Ophthalmic artery (*A. ophthalmic*
24. Site for hypophysis (*Sella turcica*
25. Posterior cerebral artery (*A. cerebri posterior*)
26. Basilar artery (*A. basilaris*)
27. Glossopharyngeal and vagus nerve (*Nn. glossopharyngeus et vagus*)
28. Inferior superficial cerebellar vein (*Vv. cerebelli inferiores super-ficiales*)
29. Posterior inferior cerebellar artery (*A. cerebelli inferior posterior*)
30. Anterior inferior cerebellar artery (*A. cerebelli inferior anterior*)
31. Lateral superior cerebellar vein (*V. cerebelli superior lateralis*)
32. Trochlear nerve (*N. trochlearis*)
33. Posterior communicating artery (*A. communicans posterior*)
34. Hypophysis (*Hypophysis*)
35. Sylvian vein (*V. cerebri media*)
36. Anterior communicating artery (*A. communicans anterior*)
37. Olfactory bulb and nerves (*Bulbus olfactorius et nervi*)

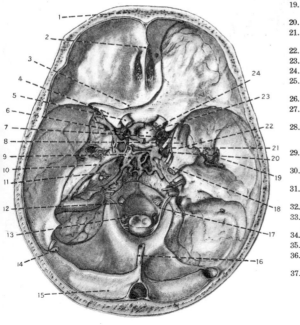

BASE OF SKULL

NAMES OF PARTS

. Right auricle (*Atrium dextrum*)
. Right ventricle (*Ventriculus dexter*)
. Pulmonary artery (*A. pulmonalis*)
. Pulmonary capillaries (*Rete pulmonale*)
. Pulmonary veins (*Vv. pulmonales*)
. Left auricle (*Atrium sinistrum*)
. Left ventricle (*Ventriculus sinister*)
. Aortic arch (*Arcus aortae*)
. Arteries of head and upper limb
   (*Arteriae capitis et extremitatis superioris*)
. Descending aorta (*Aorta descendens*)
. Internal iliac artery (*A. iliaca interna*)
. Arteries of lower limb
   (*Arteriae extremitatis inferioris*)
. Internal iliac vein (*V. iliaca interna*)
. Veins of lower limbs
   (*Venae extremitatis inferioris*)
. Inferior vena cava (*V. cava inferior*)
. Celiac trunk (*Truncus coeliacus*)
. Superior mesenteric artery
   (*A. mesenterica superior*)
. Inferior mesenteric artery
   (*A. mesenterica inferior*)
. Portal circulation (*Systema venae portae*)
. Capillaries of liver (*Rete hepatis*)
. Hepatic veins (*Venae hepaticae*)
. Superior vena cava (*V. cava superior*)

SCHEMA OF CIRCULATION

The above scheme diagrams the circulation channels. Notice the course that the blood may take coming into the right auricle (1); it passes to the right ventricle (2), and from this chamber via the pulmonary artery (3) to the lung capillaries which coalesce to form the pulmonary veins (5) that empty into the left auricle (6). From this chamber the blood passes to the left ventricle (7) and then via the aorta (8) to various parts of the organism. One will note the vessels to head and upper extremities (9), those to lower extremities (12), those to various organs of abdomen and particularly the portal circulation (19) which is a venous system bringing blood from areas of the digestive tract to the liver. Finally the capillaries of various parts fuse into veins (15, 22) that enter the right auricle (1)

126

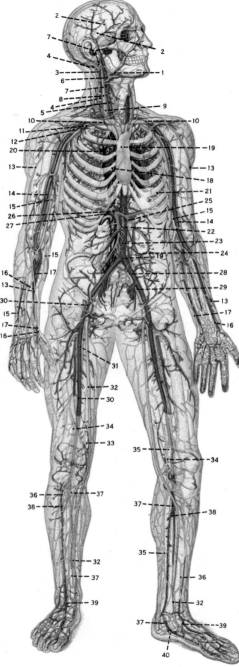

NAMES OF PARTS

1. External maxillary (*A. maxillaris exter*
2. Middle meningeal (*A. meningea media*
3. External jugular (*V. jugularis extern*
4. Vertebral (*A. vertebralis*)
5. Common carotid (*A. carotis communis*
6. External carotid (*A. carotis externa*)
7. Internal carotid (*A. carotis interna*)
8. Internal jugular (*V. jugularis interna*
9. Bulb of jugular (*Bulbus V. jugularis*)
10. Subclavian (*A. subclavia*)
11. Subclavian (*V. subclavia*)
12. Axillary (*A. et. V. axillaris*)
13. Cephalic (*V. cephalica*)
14. Brachial (*A. brachialis*)
15. Basilic (*V. basilica*)
16. Radial (*A. radialis*)
17. Ulnar (*A. ulnaris*)
18. Heart (*Cor*)
19. Aorta (*Aorta*)
20. Superior vena cava (*V. cava superior*)
21. Intercostal (*A. intercostalis*)
22. Superior mesenteric
    (*A et V. mesenterica superior*)
23. Inferior mesenteric
    (*A. mesenterica inferior*)
24. Sigmoid (*A. et V. sigmoidales*)
25. Inferior mesenteric
    (*V. mesenterica inferior*)
26. Portal (*V. portae*)
27. Right renal (*A. et V. renalis dextra*)
28. Common iliac (*A. et V. iliaca commun*
29. External iliac (*A. et V. iliaca externa*
30. Femoral (*A. et V. femoralis*)
31. Deep femoral (*A. et V. profunda femo*
32. Large saphenous (*V. saphena magna*)
33. Lateral superior artery of knee
    (*A. genus superior lateralis*)
34. Popliteal (*A. et V. poplitea*)
35. Small saphenous (*V. saphena parva*)
36. Anterior tibial (*A. et V. tibialis anter*
37. Posterior tibial (*A. tibialis posterior*)
38. Peroneal (*A. peronaea*)
39. Dorsal (*A. et V. dorsalis pedis*)
40. Medial plantar (*A. plantaris medialis*

Other illustrations in this at
showing the parts on a larger sc
give more detailed information t
is possible in this generalized ch
of the whole system.

The location of main arterie
protected areas should be observ
also that main arterial and ven
trunks are parallel.

THE CIRCULATION SYSTEM
BLOOD VESSELS

NAMES OF PARTS—Figs. 1, 2, 3 and 4

Brachiocephalic (*A. brachiocephalica*)
Left common carotid (*A. carotis sinistra*)
Left subclavian (*A. subclavia sinistra*)
Ascending aorta (*Aorta ascendéns*)
Arch of aorta (*Arcus aortae*)
Arterial ligament (*L. arteriosum*)
Pulmonary (*A. pulmonalis*)
Right pulmonary (*Aa. pulmonales dextrae*)
Left pulmonary (*A. pulmonalis sinistra*)
Superior vena cava (*V. cava superior*)
Inferior vena cava (*V. cava inferior*)
Oval fossa (*Fossa ovalis*)
Eustachian valve (*Valvula V. cavae*)
Valve of coronary sinus (*Valvula sinus coronarii*)
Right coronary (*A. coronaria dextra*)
Left coronary (*A. coronaria sinistra*)
Great cardiac vein (*V. cordis magna*)
Right ventricle (*Ventriculus dexter*)
Interventricular septum (*Septum ventriculorum*)
Papillary muscles (*Mm. papillares*)
Tricuspid valve (*Valvulae tricuspidalis—Cuspis anterior*)
Arterial cone (*Conus arteriosus*)
Right anterior pulmonary semilunar valve (*Valvula dextra lunares arteriae pulmonalis*)
Left anterior (*Valvula sinistra*)
Posterior (*Valvula posterior*)
Left auricle (*Auricula sinistra*)
Left atrium (*Atrium sinistrum*)
Right pulmonary (*Vv. pulmonales dextrae*)
Left pulmonary (*Vv. pulmonales sinistrae*)
Coronary sinus (*Sinus coronarius*)
Bicuspid valve. anterior cusp (*Cuspis anterior valvulae bicuspidalis*)
(*Cuspis posterior*)
Left ventricle (*Ventriculus sinister*)
33a, 33b. Aortic semilunar valves (*Valvulae semilunares aortae*)
Apex of Heart (*Apex cordis*)

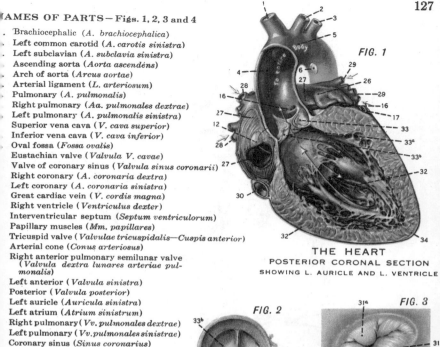

THE HEART
POSTERIOR CORONAL SECTION
SHOWING L. AURICLE AND L. VENTRICLE

FIG. 2
AORTIC VALVE

FIG. 3
MITRAL VALVE
OR
BICUSPID VALVE

The student should compare the illustrations in figures 1 and 4 with the diagram on page 125 and trace the arrows, naming the parts through which the blood passes. Note also the greater thickness of the left ventricular wall than that of the right ventricle. Notice in figure 4 that only a margin of the left ventricle can be seen; the right ventricle faces forward in the chest.

The valves shown in figures 2 and 3 are closed. Note the open semilunar in figure 1 and the open tricuspid in figure 4.

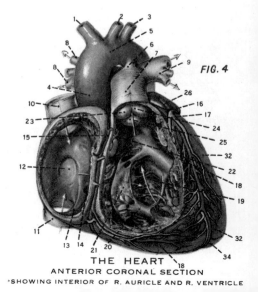

THE HEART
ANTERIOR CORONAL SECTION
SHOWING INTERIOR OF R. AURICLE AND R. VENTRICLE

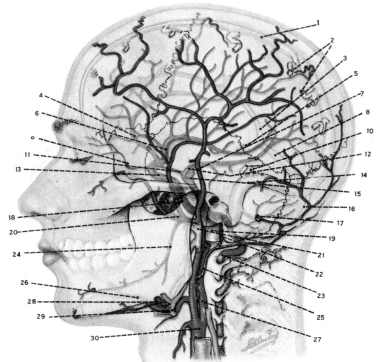

CIRCULATION SYSTEM OF THE HEAD

NAMES OF PARTS

1. Superior sagittal sinus
   (*Sinus sagittalis superior*)
2. Superior cerebral veins
   (*Vv. cerebri superiores*)
3. Inferior sagittal sinus
   (*Sinus sagittalis inferior*)
4. Anterior cerebral artery
   (*A. cerebri anterior*)
5. Vein of Galen.
   (*V. Galeni, v. cerebri magna*)
6. Middle cerebral artery (*A. cerebri media*)
7. Superficial temporary artery
   (*A. temporalis superficialis*)
8. Straight sinus (*Sinus rectus*)
9. Ophthalmic artery (*A. ophthalmica*)
10. Cerebral veins (*Vv. cerebri*)
11. Posterior communicating artery
    (*A. communicans posterior*)
12. Posterior cerebral arteries
    (*Aa. cerebri posteriores*)
13. Internal carotid artery
    (*A. carotis interna*)
14. Lateral sinus (*Sinus transversus*)
15. Basilar artery (*A. basilaris*)

16. Occipital sinus (*Sinus occipitalis*)
17. Mastoid foramen, artery and vein
    (*Foramen mastoideum, A. et. V.*)
18. Middle meningeal artery
    (*A. meningea media*)
19. Internal jugular vein
    (*V. jugularis interna*)
20. Internal maxillary artery
    (*A. maxillaris interna*)
21. External jugular vein and external carotid artery
    (*V. jugularis externa et. A. carotis externa*)
22. Posterior meningeal artery
    (*A. meningea posterior*)
23. Vertebral artery and venous plexus
    (*A. vertebralis et vv. plexus*)
24. Inferior alveolar artery
    (*A. alveolaris inferior*)
25. Occipital artery (*A. occipitalis*)
26. Lingual artery (*A. lingualis*)
27. Internal carotid artery
    (*A. carotis interna*)
28. External maxillary artery
    (*A. maxillaris externa*)
29. Common facial vein (*V. facialis communis*)
30. Common carotid artery
    (*A. carotis communis*)

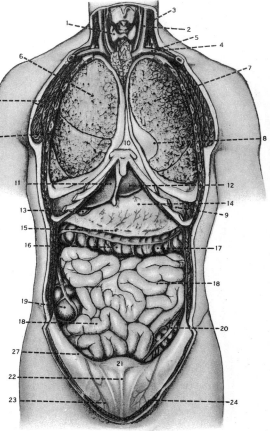

NAMES OF PARTS

Thyroid gland (*Gl. thyreoidea*)
Internal jugular (*V. jugularis interna*)
Sternocleido-mastoid
  (*M. sternocleido-mastoideus*)
Subclavian (*A. et V. subclavia*)
Thymus (*Thymus*)
Right lung (*Pulmo dexter*)
Left lung (*Pulmo sinister*)
Cardiac notch (*Incisura cardiaca*)
Diaphragm (*Diaphragma*)
Pericardium (*Pericardium*)
Right lobe liver (*Lobus dexter hepatis*)
Left lobe liver (*Lobus sinister hepatis*)
Gall bladder (*Vesica fellea*)
Stomach (*Ventriculus*)
Greater omentum (cut edge)
  (*Omentum majus*)
Transverse colon (*Colon transversum*)
Sacculation of colon (*Haustrum coli*)
Small intestine (*Intestinum tenue*)
Blind intestine (*Caecum*)
Sigmoid (*Colon sigmoideum*)
Bladder (*Vesica urinaria*)
Medial umbilical fold
  (*Plica umbilicalis media*)
Inferior epigastric
  (*A. epigastrica inferior*)
Straight muscle (*M. rectus abdominis*)
Greater pectoral muscle
  (*M. pectoralis major*)
Intercostal muscles ((*Mm. intercostales*)
Peritoneum (*Peritonaeum*)

VISCERA OF CHEST AND ABDOMEN
FIRST LAYER

The term viscera is used to designate the organs of the chest and abdomen. The above illustration shows the appearance of the chest and abdominal cavities with the wall covering removed and, in the abdomen a layer of fatty tissue, called the omentum, also cut away. In these and other organs lies the vitality of an individual and hence the term vital organs, often used. Notice that the left lung almost entirely covers the heart, the projection of the liver below the ribs, and the coiled intestines below the stomach.

The maintenance of a vigorous circulation through these organs, supplying nourishment and removing waste, is directly dependent upon heart action. Improved functioning of the vital organs following physical exercise is in part due to an improved circulation and in part a reflection of increased demands upon these organs by the muscles.

Note particularly the thyroid as indicated above (1) and the posterior view of it (17) on page 136. Observe that the liver extends a considerable distance to the left of the midline.

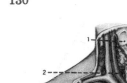

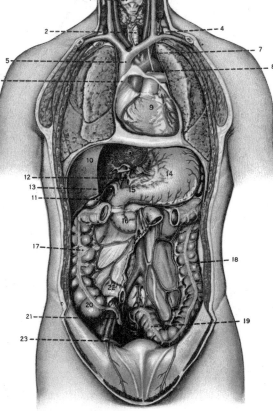

NAMES OF PARTS

1. Thyroid cartilage
   (*Cartilago thyreoidea*)
2. Windpipe (*Trachea*)
3. Left common carotid
   (*A. carotis communis sinistr*
4. Thoracic duct (*Ductus thoraci*
5. Superior cava (*V. cava superi*
6. Pericardium (*Pericardium*)
7. Phrenic (*N. phrenicus*)
8. Vagus (*N. vagus*)
9. Heart (*Cor*)
10. Liver (*Hepar*)
11. Gall bladder (*Vessica fellea*)
12. Hepatic artery, portal vein,
    hepatic duct (*A. hepatica pr
    V. portae, ductus hepaticus*)
13 Foramen of Winslow
   (*Foramen epiploicum*)
14. Stomach (*Ventriculus*)
15. Pylorus (*Pylorus*)
16. Duodenum (*Duodenum*)
17. Ascending colon (*Colon ascend*
18. Descending colon *Colon desce*
19. Sigmoid (*Colon sigmoideum*)
20. Blind intestine (*Caecum*)
21. Appendix (*Processus vermifor*
22. Ileum (*Ileum*)
23. Spermatic duct (*Ductus defere*

VISCERA OF CHEST AND ABDOMEN
SECOND LAYER

In this dissection, the first layer of viscera is removed. The small intestine, except the first twelve inches (duodenum), and the transverse colon are lifted out. The lungs are turned sideward, and the front wall of the pericardium is dissected out, exposing the heart. Notice the appendix hanging from the lower end of the caecum. Notice, too, that at the lower margin of the abdomen there is a central swelling, constituting the fundus of the bladder.

In the above illustration notice the thick muscles of the chest walls, the liver (10) cut away to expose the stomach (14). The large colon with its sacculations presents a structure quite different in form from the small intestine (16) as shown on page 129.

NAMES OF PARTS

Vertebral (*A. vertebralis*)
Brachiocephalic
  (*A. brachiocephalica*)
Aortic arch (*Arcus aortae*)
Superior cava (*V. cava superior*)
Left vagus (*N. vagus sinister*)
Pulmonary (*A. pulmonalis*)
Pulmonary vessels and bronchii
  (*Vasa pulmonalia et bronchii*)
Pleura (*Pleura*)
Diaphragm (*Diaphragma*)
Cardiac end of stomach (*Cardia*)
Hepatic veins (*Vv. hepaticae*)
Inferior cava (*V. cava inferior*)
Celiac (*Truncus coeliacus*)
Spleen and splenic vessels
  (*Lien et vasa lienalia*)
Right suprarenal gland
  (*Glandula suprarenalis dextra*)
Right kidney (*Ren dexter*)
Left kidney (*Ren sinister*)
Ureter (*Ureter*)
Pancreas (*Pancreas*)
Duodenojejunal flexure
  (*Flexura duodenojejunalis*)
Abdominal aorta (*Aorta abdominalis*)
Inferior mesenteric
  (*A. mesenterica inferior*)
Femoral nerve (*N. femoralis*)
Common iliac (*A. et V. iliaca communis*)
External iliac (*A. et V. iliaca externa*)
Rectum (*Rectum*)

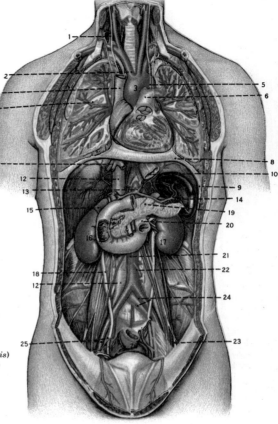

VISCERA OF CHEST AND ABDOMEN
THIRD LAYER

In this view of the third layer numerous organs are removed. The thyroid in the neck, stomach, liver, and colon are gone. The lungs and heart have been dissected to expose the internal structure of each. In the abdomen, the duodenum is left to indicate its relationship with the head of the pancreas. This view shows for the first time the spleen, the kidneys, ureters and pancreas. Compare the vessels and nerves in this illustration with those on pages 129, 130 and 132.

This dissection shows clearly the two main cavities of the trunk: the chest above the diaphragm, and the abdomen below. The cut edge of the diaphragm is seen clearly with the heart and lungs resting upon its upper surface.

The abdominal aorta divides into two iliac arteries and provides circulation for the pelvic region and lower extremities. Compare with illustration on page 126.

132

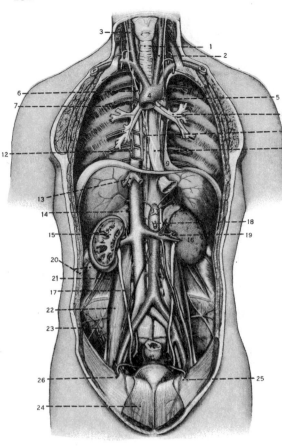

NAMES OF PARTS

1. Windpipe (*Trachea*)
2. Left common carotid
   (*A. carotis communis sinist*)
3. Right common carotid
   (*A. carotis communis dextr*)
4. Aortic arch (*Arcus aortae*)
5. Left vagus (*N. vagus sinister*)
6. Right vagus ((*N. vagus dexter*)
7. Intercostal nerves and vessels
   (*Nn. et Vasa intercostales*)
8. Left bronchus and bronchial a
   (*Bronchus sinister et A. bro*)
9. Costal pleura (*Pleura costalis*)
10. Thoracic duct (*Ductus thoraci*)
11. Gullet (*Oesophagus*)
12. Sympathetic trunk
    (*Truncus sympatheticus*)
13. Hepatic veins (*Vv. hepaticae*)
14. Suprarenal gland
    (*Glandula suprarenalis*)
15. Renal calices (*Calices renales*)
16. Left kidney (*Ren sinister*)
17. Ureter (*Ureter*)
18. Superior mesenteric
    (*A. mesenterica superior*)
19. Kidney vessels (*Vasa renalia*)
20. Tranverse muscle
    (*M. transversus abdominis*)
21. Quadrate muscle
    (*M. quadratus lumborum*)
22. Greater psoas muscle
    (*M. psoas major*)
23. Iliac muscle (*M. iliacus*)
24. Straight muscle
    (*M. rectus abdominis*)
25. Ligament of Hesselbach
    (*L. interfoveolare*)
26. Inguinal ring
    (*Annulus inguinalis*)

VISCERA OF CHEST AND ABDOMEN
FOURTH LAYER

The fourth layer of the viscera brings the dissection to the posterior wall. In the chest cavity, only trachea, bronchi, and vessels remain. Notice the oesophagus and its opening below the diaphragm. The two kidneys receiving blood from the two large renal arteries, are capped by adrenals, glands of internal secretion.

The peritoneum has been removed and the muscles exposed. Note the greater psoas muscle, its size and position.

On the right side (15) the kidney is dissected to show something of its internal structure. From the cells of this organ the secretion, urine, is passed into the ureter (17) finally reaching the bladder (21) as numbered on page 129.

Notice also the internal inguinal ring (26) with the spermatic cord indicated on its way to the scrotum.

NAMES OF PARTS

Orifice of Stenson's duct
  (Orificium ducti parotidei)
Orifice of Wharton's duct
  (Orificium ducti submaxillaris)
Sub-Lingual gland *(Gl. sublingualis)*
Parotid gland *(Gl. parotis)*
Submandibular gland
  (Gl. submandibularis)
Epiglottis *(Epiglottis)*
Pharynx *(Pharynx)*
Vocal cord *(Plica vocalis)*
Larynx *(Larynx)*
Gullet *(Oesophagus)*
Gall-bladder *(Vesica fellea)*
Liver *(Hepar)*
Stomach *(Ventriculus)*
Pancreas *(Pancreas)*
Pylorus *(Pylorus)*
Orifice of Santorini duct
  (Orificium ducti pancreatici accessorii)
Splenic flexure of colon
  (Flexura coli sinistra)
Hepatic flexure of colon
  (Flexura coli dextra)
Orifice of bile and pancreatic ducts
  (Orificium ducti choledochi et ducti pancreatici)
Jejunum *(Intestinum jejunum)*
Ileum *(Intestinum ileum)*
Caecum and appendix
  (Intestinum caecum et processus vermiformis)
Sigmoid flexure of colon
  (Flexura coli sigmoidea)
Levator ani muscle
  (M. levator ani)
External sphincter ani muscle
  (M. sphincter ani externus)

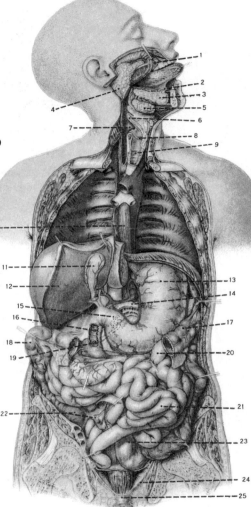

ALIMENTARY TRACT

The above illustration presents a view of the alimentary tract from mouth to anus. The relationship with glands along the way is indicated. Notice the salivary glands in the mouth (3, 4, 5) and the opening (19) in the duodenum of the duct, from the liver (12) and the pancreas (14) By removing portions of the pelvis the lower end of the sigmoid colon and rectum are brought into view.

Note particularly the liver turned upward to show the gall bladder (11), the appendix (22), the pancreas (14) lying behind the stomach, and the chest cavity from which the lungs and heart have been removed.

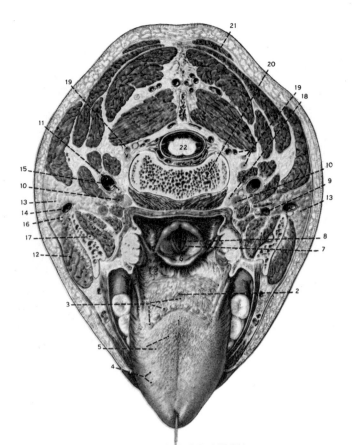

SECTION· OF NECK

THE SECTION IS HORIZONTAL THROUGH SECOND CERVICAL VERTEBRA

1. Dorsum of tongue (*Dorsum linguae*)
2. Foramen caecum
    (*Foramen caecum linguae*)
3. Circumvallate papillae (*Papillae vallatae*)
4. Fungiform papillae
    (*Papillae fungiformes*)
5. Filiform and conical papillae
    (*Papillae filiformes et conicae*)
6. Epiglottis (*Epiglottis*)
7. False vocal chord (*Plica ventricularis*)
8. True vocal chord (*Plica vocalis*)
9. External carotid (*A. carotis externus*)
10. Internal carotid (*A carotis internus*)
11. Right vagus (*N. vagus dexter*)

12. Masseter (*M. masseter*)
13. Parotid gland (*Gl. parotis*)
14. External jugular (*V. jugularis externa*)
15. Internal jugular (*V. jugularis interna*)
16. Facial (*N. facialis*)
17. Inferior dental (*N. alveolaris inferior*)
18. Superior cervical ganglion
    (*Ggl. cervicale superius*)
19. Vertebral artery and veins
    (*A. et. Vv. vertebrales*)
20. Second cervical vertebra (*Axis*)
21. Trapezius (*M. trapezius*)
22. Spinal cord (*Medulla spinalis*)

This illustration shows the structures met in a section through the level of the lower jaw. The central position of the spine (20) is strikingly observed. and the position of the spinal cord (22) in the canal behind the body of the cervical vertebra. The view of the larynx and epiglottis (6) from above showing the vocal chords (7, 8) is unusual.

NAMES OF PARTS

1. Uvula (*Uvula*)
2. Posterior wall pharynx (*Isthmus faucium*)
3. Gums (*Gingivae*)
4. Soft palate (*Palatum molle*)
5. Middle incisor (*Dens incisivus medialis*)
6. Lateral incisor (*Dens incisivus lateralis*)
7. Canine (*Dens caninus*)
8. Premolars (*Dentes praemolares*)
9. Bicuspids (*Dentes praemolares*)
10. Molars (*Dentes molares*)
11. Molars (*Dentes molares*)
12. Wisdom (*Dens serotinus*)
13. Gasserian ganglion (*Ggl. semilunare*)
14. Ophthalmic (*N. ophthalmicus*)
15. Maxillary (*N. maxillaris*)
16. Mandibular (*N. mandibularis*)
17. Posterior superior dental
   (*Rami alveolares superiores posteriores*)
18. Infraorbital (*N. infraorbitalis*)
19. Mucous membrane of antrum
   (*Tunica mucosa, sinus maxillaris*)
20. Inferior dental (*N. alveolaris inferior*)
21. Lingual (*N. lingualis*)
22. Chorda tympani (*Chorda tympani*)
23. Tonsil (*Tonsilla*)

THE MOUTH CAVITY
CHEEKS HAVE BEEN CUT TO ALLOW
DISTENTION OF JAWS

These two views give other interesting details of the mouth and head region. Above notice the position of the tonsils (23).

In the lower illustration the distribution of nerves to the teeth is clearly shown. These nerves all come from the 5th cranial nerve.

Particular note should be taken of the close relationship of the teeth of the upper jaw to the maxillary sinus (19). Infection from these teeth may extend into the antrum.

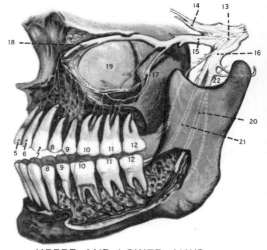

UPPER AND LOWER JAWS
LATERAL VIEW
THE NERVES OF THE TEETH ARE SHOWN IN THE
UPPER JAW AND THE BLOOD VESSELS IN THE LOWER

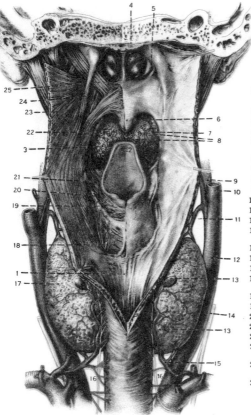

1. Mucous membrane of esophagus
   (*Tunica mucosa oesophagi*)
2. Epiglottis (*Epiglottis*)
3. Tongue (*Lingua*)
4. Posterior nares (*Choanae*)
5. Eustachian tube
   (*Ostium pharyngeum tubae auditiva*)
6. Uvula (*Uvula*)
7. Tonsil (*Tonsilla*)
8. Circumvallate papillae (*Papillae vallat*)
9. External carotid (*A. carotis externa*)
10. Internal carotid (*A. carotis interna*)
11. Superior thyroid (*A. thyreoidea super*)
12. Common carotid ((*A. carotis communi*)
13. Parathyroid gland
    (*Glandula parathyreoidea*)
14. Right vagus (*N. vagus dexter*)
15. Inferior thyroid (*A. thyreoidea inferior*)
16. Recurrent (*N. recurrens*)
17. Left lobe of thyroid gland
    (*Lobus sinister glandulae thyreoidea*)
18. Inferior laryngeal (*N. laryngeus infer*)
19. Aryepiglotticus (*M. ary-epiglotticus*)
20. Superior laryngeal (*N.laryngeus super*)
21. Stylo-pharyngeus (*M. stylo-pharyngeu*)
22. Root of tongue (*Radix linguae*)
23. Superior constrictor pharynx
    (*M. constrictor pharyngis superior*)
24. Salpingo pharyngeus
    (*M. salpingopharyngeus*)
25. Levator palate (*M. levator veli palatin*)

SECTION OF NECK
Coronal
THIS VIEW IS FROM BEHIND   THE PHARYNX HAS
BEEN CUT OPEN

This very unusual view shows the throat as viewed from the back. The two small "eyes" (4) above are the opening from the nasal passageways into the upper pharynx. Below is the opening from the mouth with the uvula (6) viewed from the rear instead of the front (1) as in fig. 1

Below this is the oval structure—the epiglottis (2) riding the larynx. Notice that the pharynx is a common passageway for food to the stomach via the oesophagus (1) and the air to the lungs via the larynx. The lateral lobes of the thyroid (17) swinging from the front are shown and the small bean shaped bodies of the parathyroids (13).

The abundant blood supply to the thyroid is shown. In some conditions of goiter, ligation of some vessels to the organ results in decreased activity of the gland.

THE HUMAN EAR

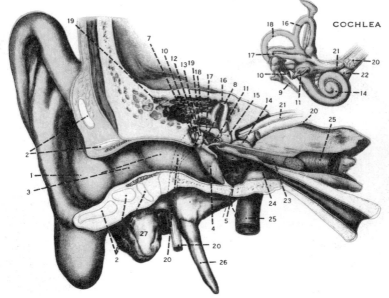

COCHLEA

NAMES OF PARTS

1. External ear (*Auricula*)
2. Cartilage of auricle (*Cartilago auriculae*)
3. External auditory meatus
   (*Meatus acousticus externus*)
4. Ear drum (*Membrana tympani*)
5. Tympanic cavity (*Cavum tympani*)
6. Promontory (*Promontorium*)
7. Epitympanic recess
   (*Recessus epitympanicus*)
8. Superior recess of tympanic membrane
   (*Recessus membranae tympani superior*)
9. Hammer (*Malleus*)
10. Anvil (*Incus*)
11. Stirrup (*Stapes*)
12. Lateral ligament of hammer
    (*L. mallei laterale*)
13. Superior ligament of hammer
    (*L. mallei superius*)
14. Cochlea ((*Cochlea*)
15. Vestibule (*Vestibulum*)
16. Anterior semicircular canal
    (*Canalis semicircularis anterior*)
17. Lateral semicircular canal
    (*Canalis semicircularis lateralis*)
18. Posterior semicircular canal
    (*Canalis semicircularis posterior*)
19. Tympanic antrum (*Antrum tympanicum*)
20. Facial nerve (*N. facialis*)
21. Vestibular nerve (*N. vestibularis*)
22. Cochlear nerve (*N. cochlearis*)
23. Tensor of tympanum (*M. tensor tympani*)
24. Bony part of Eustachian tube
    (*Pars ossea tubae auditivae*)
25. Internal carotid (*A. carotis interna*)
26. Styloid process (*Processus styloideus*)
27. Mastoid process (*Processus mastoideus*)

This section, through the auditory apparatus, is excellent. It shows the canal with the drum membrane (4), the middle ear in which the ear ossicles (9, 10, 11) are situated and the Eustachian tube (24) connecting with the pharynx. Notice the close relationship of the facial nerve (20), to the mastoid process (27).

In mastoid operation the surgeon needs to skillfully avoid injury to this nerve, which supplies muscles of the face. The ending of the auditory nerve in the cochlea (14), the organ of hearing, and the canals (16, 17, 18) are shown in the enlarged insert.

LEFT HUMAN EYE
SECTION

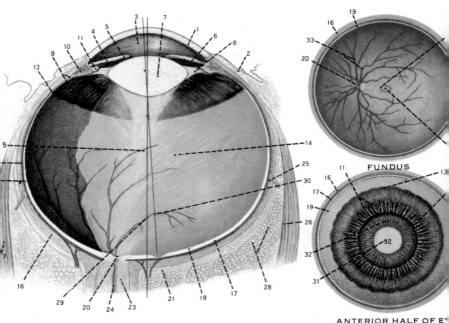

FUNDUS

ANTERIOR HALF OF EY
VIEWED FROM BEHIND

NAMES OF PARTS

1. Cornea (*Cornea*)
2. Conjunctiva (*Conjunctiva bulbi*)
3. Anterior chamber
 (*Camera oculi anterior*)
4. Iris (*Iris*)
5. Sphincter of pupil (*Sphincter pupillae*)
6. Posterior chamber
 (*Camera oculi posterior*)
7. Crystalline lens (*Lens crystallina*)
8. Ciliary zonule (*Zonula ciliaris*)
9. Ciliary body (*Corpus ciliare*)
10. Ciliary muscle (*M. ciliares*)
11. Ciliary processes (*Processus ciliares*)
12. Ciliary folds (*Plicae ciliares*)
13. Serrated edge (*Ora serrata*)
14. Vitreous body (*Corpus vitreum*)
15. Hyaloid canal (*Canalis hyaloideus*)
16. Sclera (*Sclera*)
17. Choroid (*Choroidea*)
18. Pigment layer retina
 (*Stratum pigmenti retinae*)
19. Retina (*Retina*)
20. Excavation of papilla
 (*Excavatio papillae nervi optici*)
21. Central fovea (*Fovea centralis*)
22. Yellow spot (*Macula lutea*)
23. Optic nerve (*N. opticus*)
24. Central vessels (*Vasa centralia retinae*)
25. Vortex vein (*V. vorticosa*)
26. Lateral straight muscle
 (*M. rectus oculi lateralis*)
27. Medial straight muscle
 (*M. rectus oculi medialis*)
28. Fat of orbit (*Corpus adiposum orbitae*)
29. Optic axis (*Axis optica*)
30. Line of vision (*Linea visus*)
31. Pupil (*Pupilla*)
32. Posterior surface of iris
 (*Facies posterior iridis*)
33. Vessels of retina
 (*Vasa sanguinea retinae*)

The eye is merely an arrangement for receiving light rays upon a sensitive surface, the retina (19), studded with nerve cells. A shutter arrangement (4) opens and closes partially to take in more or exclude light rays. In addition a lens (7), adjustable automatically, brings the light rays to a focus on the retina so the image produced is clear. From the stimulation of receptors by the image, the impulse passes to the brain and sight takes place.

NAMES OF PARTS

1. Testicle (*Testis*)
2. Spermatic cord (*Funiculus spermaticus*)
3. Glans (*Glans penis*)
4. Foreskin (*Praeputium*)
5. Membranous urethra
   (*Pars membrananea urethrae*)
6. Inner structure testis (*Parenchyma testis*)
7. Penis (*Penis*)
8. Epididymis (*Epididymis*)
9. Efferent ducts (*Ductuli efferentes testis*)
9. Duct Cowper's gland
   (*Ductus glandulae bulbo-urethralis*)
. Spongy body
   (*Corpus spongiosum penis*)
. Vas deferens (*Ductus deferens*)
. Ejaculatory duct (*Ductus ejaculatorius*)
. Prostatic utricle (*Utriculus prostaticus*)
. Bladder (*Vesica urinaria*)
. Ureteral orifice (*Orificium ureteris*)
. Triangle of bladder (*Trigonum vesicae*)
. Venous plexus of prostate
   (*Plexus prostaticus*)
. Prostate (*Prostata*)
. Orifices prostatic ducts
   (*Orificia ductuli prostatici*)
. Cavernous body of penis
   (*Corpus cavernosum penis*)
. Spermatic fascia
   (*Fascia spermatica interna*)
. Parietal tunica vaginalis (*Tunica vaginalis propria testis—lamina parietalis*)
. Visceral tunica vaginalis (*Tunica vaginalis propria testis—lamina visceralis*)
. Appendix epididymis
   (*Appendix epididymidis*)

26. Appendix testis
    (*Appendix testis—Morgagnii*)
27. Skin (*Cutis*)
28. Ureter (*Ureter*)
29. Vas deferens (*Ductus deferens*)
30. Ampulla of vas
    (*Ampulla ductus deferentis*)
31. Seminal vesicle (*Vesicula seminalis*)
32. Middle muscular coat of bladder
    (*Tunicae muscularis stratum medium*)
33. Superficial muscular coat
    (*Tunicae muscularis stratum externum*)
34. Levator ani muscle (*M. levator ani*)
35. Ischio-cavernosous muscle
    (*M. ischio-cavernosus*)
41. Muscular coat of bladder
    (*Tunica muscularis*)

POSTERIOR VIEW
OF BLADDER, SEMINAL VESICLES
PROSTATE AND VAS DEFERENS

UROGENITAL ORGANS—MALE

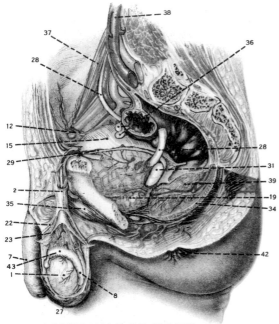

LEFT HALF OF PELVIS
SAGITTAL SECTION SHOWING GENITO-URINARY TRACT

NAMES OF PARTS

1. Testicle (*Testis*)
2. Spermatic cord (*Funiculus spermaticus*)
3. Glans (*Glans penis*)
4. Foreskin (*Praeputium*)
5. Membranous urethra (*Pars membrana urethrae*)
7. Penis (*Penis*)
8. Epididymis (*Epididymis*)
10. Duct Cowper's gland (*Ductus excretorius glandulae bulbo-urethralis*)
11. Spongy body (*Corpus spongiosum penis*)
12. Vas deferens (*Ductus deferens*)
13. Ejaculatory duct (*Ductus ejaculatorius*)
14. Prostatic utricle (*Utriculus prostaticus*)
15. Bladder (*Vesica urinaria*)
16. Ureteral orifice (*Orificium ureter*
19. Prostate (*Prostata*)
22. Internal spermatic fascia (*Fascia spermatica interna*)
23. Parietal tunica vaginalis (*Tunica vaginalis propria test lamina parietalis*)
27. Skin (*Cutis*)
28. Ureter (*Ureter*)
29. Vas deferens (*Ductus deferens*)
30. Ampulla of vas (*Ampulla ductus deferentis*)
31. Seminal vesicle (*Vesicula semino*
34. Levator ani muscle (*M. levator a*
35. Ischio-cavernosus muscle (*M. ischio cavernosus*)
36. Epiploic appendages (*Appendices epiploicae*)
37. Psoas muscle (*M. psoas*)
38. Abdominal aorta (*A. aorta abdominalis*)
39. Rectum (*Intestinum rectum*)
40. Fossanavicularis (*Fossa navicularis*)
41. Muscular coat of bladder (*Tunica muscularis*)
42. Anus (*Anus*)
43. Head of epididymis (*Caput epididymidis*)

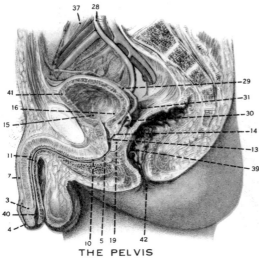

THE PELVIS
MEDIAN SAGITTAL SECTION SHOWING GENITO-URINARY TRACT

UROGENITAL ORGANS—FEMALE

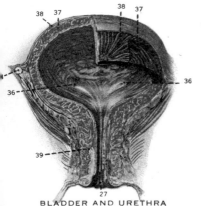

NAMES OF PARTS

1. Ampulla of tube
   (*Ampulla tubae uterinae,*
2. Fimbriae (*Fimbriae tubae*)
3. Suspensory ligament of ovary
   (*L. suspensorium ovarii*)
4. Ovary (*Ovarium*)
5. Meso-salpinx (*Mesosalpinx*)
6. Corpus luteum (*Corpus luteum*)
7. Utero-ovarian ligament
   (*L. ovarii proprium*)
8. Uterus (*Uterus*)
9. Serous coat (*Tunica serosa*)
10. Muscular coat (*Tunica muscularis*)
11. Mucous coat (*Tunica mucosa*)
12. Uterine end of tube
    (*Ostium uterinum tubae*)
13. Fallopian tube (*Tuba uterina*)
14. Ovarian artery and vein
    (*A. et. V. ovarii*)
15. Hydatid of Morgagni
    (*Appendix vesiculosa*)
16. Graafian follicle
    (*Folliculus oophorus vesiculosus*)
17. Primordial follicles
    (*Folliculi oophorii primarii*)
18. Corpus albicans (*Corpus albicans*)
19. Ureter (*Ureter*)
20. Cervix (*Cervix uteri*)
21. Vagina (*Vagina*)
22. Symphysis pubis
    (*Symphysis ossium pubis*)
23. Bladder (*Vesica urinaria*)
24. Lateral umbilical ligament
    (*L. umbilicale laterale*)
25. Prepuce (*Praeputium clitoridis*)
26. Glans (*Glans clitoridis*)
27. External urethral orifice
    (*Orificium urethrae externum*)
28. Labium majus (*Labium majus pudendi*)
29. Labium minus (*Labium minus pudendi*)
30. Vaginal orifice (*Orificium vaginae*)
31. Bartholin's gland
    (*Orificium glandulae vestibularis*)
32. Fossa navicularis (*Fossa navicularis*)
33. Fourchette (*Frenulum labiorum pudendi*)
34. Anus (*Anus*)
35. Bulb (*Bulbus vestibuli*)
36. Ureteral orifice (*Orificium ureteris*)
37. Middle muscle layer
    (*Tunicae muscularis stratum medium*)
38. Superficial muscle layer
    (*Tunicae muscularis stratum externum*)
39. Skene's gland (*Glandula urethralis*)

UTERUS,
ADDER AND
NAL GENITALIA
LEFT HALF IS
DISSECTED TO DISPLAY THE INTERNAL STRUCTURE

BLADDER AND URETHRA
CUT OPEN TO SHOW INTERIOR ANTERIOR VIEW

EARLY PREGNANCY

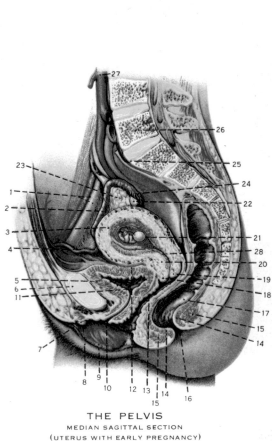

THE PELVIS

MEDIAN SAGITTAL SECTION

(UTERUS WITH EARLY PREGNANCY)

NAMES OF PARTS

1. External iliac artery and vein
   (*A. et V. iliaca externa*)
2. Fallopian tube (*Tuba uterine*)
3. Uterus (*Uterus*)
4. Round ligament (*L. teres ute*)
5. Bladder (*Vesica urinaria*)
6. Symphysis pubis
   (*Symphysis ossium pubis*)
7. Glans (*Glans clitoridis*)
8. Labium majus
   (*Labium majus pudendi*)
9. Labium minus
   (*Labium minus pudendi*)
10. External urethral orifice
    (*Orificium urethrae extern*)
11. Internal urethral orifice
    (*Orificium urethrae inter*)
12. Vesico-uterine pouch
    (*Excavatio vesico-uterina*)
13. Vagina (*Vagina*)
14. Internal sphincter ani muscle
    (*M. sphincter ani internu*)
15. External sphincter ani muscle
    (*M. sphincter ani externu*)
16. Anus (*Anus*)
17. Rectum (*Intestinum rectum*)
18. Anterior cervical lip
    (*Labium anterius*)
19. Posterior cervical lip
    (*Labium posterius*)
20. Cervix (*Cervix uteri*)
21. Amnion (*Amnion*)
22. Hydatid of Morgagni
    (*Appendix vesiculosa*)
23. Right ovary (*Ovarium dextr*)
24. Fimbriae (*Fimbriae tubae*)
25. Sacral promontory
    (*Promontorium ossis sacr*)
26. Fifth lumbar vertebra
    (*Vertebra lumbalis V*)
27. Abdominal aorta
    (*A. aorta abdominalis*)
28. Isthmus of uterus
    (*Isthmus uteri*)

This section through the female pelvis, in addition to illustrating related parts, gives the position of the embryo developing in the fundus of the uterus (3). Spermatozoa deposited in the vagina (13) pass by their own motile power into the uterus and meet an ovum in one of the tubes (2) as it descends from the ovary (23). Two cells, spermatozoon and ovum, unite and this is the beginning of the embryo. The cell resulting from the union burrows into the membrane of the uterus and begins to grow. Blood vessels of the uterus later become organized to supply nutriment and to remove waste. This process proceeds over a period of about 9 months when the embryo has become the fetus ready to be born.

PREGNANCY AT FULL TERM
(continued)

NAMES OF PARTS

erus (*Uterus*)
adder (*Vesica urinaria*)
mphysis pubis
(*Symphysis ossium pubis*)
ans (*Glans clitoridis*)
bium majus
(*Labium majus pudendi*)
bium minus
(*Labius minus pudendi*)
ternal urethral orifice
(*Orificium urethrae externuem*)
ternal urethral orifice
(*Orificium urethrae internum*)
gina (*Vagina*)
us (*Anus*)
ctum (*Intestinum rectum*)
terior cervical lip
(*Labium anterius*)
sterior cervical lip
(*Labium posterius*)
nnion (*Amnion*)
ral promontory
(*Promontorium ossis sacri*)
dominal aorta
(*A. aortae abdominalis*)
hmus of uterus
(*Isthmus uteri*)
bilical cord
(*Funiculus umbilicalis*)
er (*Hepar*)
mach (*Ventriculus*)
nsverse colon
(*Colon transversum*)
bilicus (*Umbilicus*)

RIGHT HALF OF BODY
SAGITTAL SECTION
SHOWING UTERUS AT TERM

This view shows two striking facts : the position of the fetus at term and the compression of surrounding parts. Notice the intestines pushed upward toward the diaphragm and the marked pressure upon the sigmoid colon behind and the bladder in front. The fetus presents an attitude of universal flexion. The head has entered the pelvic basin and is undergoing molding to prepare for parturition The fetus lives in a fluid medium and the membrane (21) that closes the cavity is seen below the head. As contractions of the uterine muscle occur, the molding of the head continues and pressure on the opening of the cervix (20) increases. With rupture of the membrane (21), the fluid escapes, and parturition proceeds.

The illustration shows the umbilical cord (29) which carries vessels from the fetus to the placenta. After birth of the fetus, the placenta is expelled by uterine contractions and the cord is separated from the child by the physician.

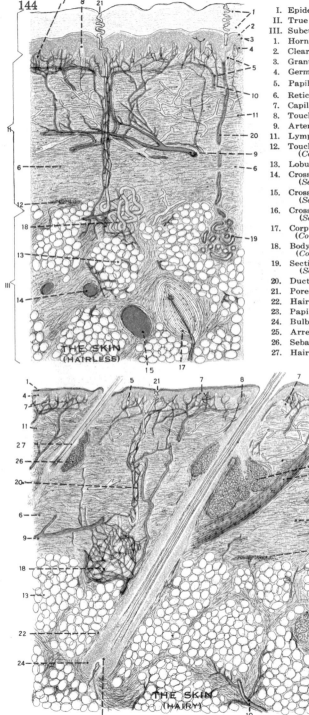

144

I. Epidermis (*Epidermis*)
II. True skin (*Corium*)
III. Subcutaneous tissue (*Tela subcutane*
1. Horny layer (*Stratum corneum*)
2. Clear layer (*Stratum lucidum*)
3. Granular layer (*Stratum granulosum*
4. Germinative layer (*Stratum germin*
5. Papillary layer of corium (*Stratum ;*
6. Reticular layer (*Stratum reticulare*)
7. Capillary network (*Rete vasculosum*
8. Touch corpuscle (*Corpusculum tacta*
9. Artery (*Arteria*). 10. Vein (*Vena*)
11. Lymphatic vessels (*Vasa lymphatica*
12. Touch corpuscle of Ruffini
(*Corpusculum tactus Ruffini*)
13. Lobules of fat (*Lobuli paniculi adip*
14. Cross section artery
(*Sectio transversa arteriae*)
15. Cross section vein
(*Sectio transversa venae*)
16. Cross section nerve
(*Sectio transversa nervi*)
17. Corpuscle of Vater
(*Corpusculum lamellosum*)
18. Body of sweat gland
(*Corpus glandulae sudoriferae*)
19. Section of sweat gland
(*Sectio glandulae sudoriferae*)
20. Duct of sweat gland (*Ductus sudori*
21. Pore of sweat gland (*Porus sudorife*
22. Hair follicle (*Folliculus pili*)
23. Papilla of a hair (*Papilla pili*)
24. Bulb of a hair (*Bulbus pili*)
25. Arrector muscle (*M. arrector pili*)
26. Sebaceous glands (*Glandulae sebace*
27. Hair falling out (*Pilus cadens*)

THE SKIN (HAIRLESS)

THE SKIN (HAIRY)

These two vie
of the skin, in
dition to details
structure, give
impression of gr
complexity. In
ality its struct
is simple. It is
sentially layers
cells that pro
against entra
of foreign s
stance into
organism, be
which are ner
blood vessels,
roots of ha
and two types
glands. Un
neath the ski
some fat in
superficial fa
covering dee
parts.

THE ENDOCRINE GLANDS

The complex activities of the whole body are under the joint control of the central nervous system and of the endocrine glands. The central nervous system is geared to almost instantaneous action by sending out nerve impulses. For this reason, it functions when immediate and, at times, lifesaving results are imperative. The endocrine glands, on the contrary, act more slowly by releasing their secretions into the blood stream to control other organs at a distance (the "target organs"). This method of control is particularly suited to long-range processes, such as growth and maturation, pregnancy, and the development of personality traits.

As stated in Chapter II, there are two kinds of glands: duct and ductless. The majority of glands in the body pour their secretions through channels or ducts to reach their objectives. Examples of organs providing such *external* or *exocrine* secretions are the salivary glands which pour saliva into the mouth in order to perform their lubricating and digestive functions. The *internal* or *endocrine* glands are ductless; their secretions, being aimed at distant targets and not at any neighboring structure, are poured directly into the blood stream. The effective chemical components of these internal secretions are termed *hormones* ("exciters" or "messengers").

Some glands are dual structures with both exocrine and endocrine secretions. Such organs have a duct for the exocrine secretion only, while the endocrine component follows the usual pattern of sending its secretion directly into the blood stream. An example is the pancreas, which pours its exocrine digestive juices into the duodenum through the pancreatic duct, while its endocrine secretion, insulin, is absorbed directly into the blood stream.

There is close interaction between the endocrine glands and the central nervous system. For example, the brain sends a nerve impulse to the pituitary gland, causing release of the appropriate pituitary secretion which, in turn, activates another gland or organ. An illustration of such cooperation is the chain reaction occurring in suckling. The stimulus arising in the breast is transmitted via the central nervous system to the pituitary gland which responds by releasing a lactation hormone to maintain and increase the flow of milk.

146

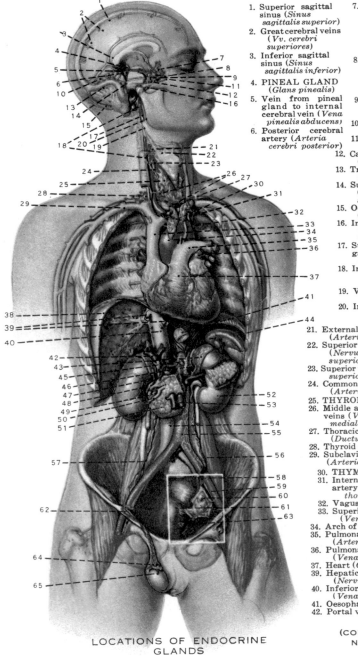

1. Superior sagittal sinus (*Sinus sagittalis superior*)
2. Great cerebral veins (*Vv. cerebri superiores*)
3. Inferior sagittal sinus (*Sinus sagittalis inferior*)
4. PINEAL GLAND (*Glans pinealis*)
5. Vein from pineal gland to internal cerebral vein (*Vena pinealis abducens*)
6. Posterior cerebral artery (*Arteria cerebri posterior*)
7. Posterior communicating artery branches to physis (*Arteria poste... et rami ad ...physim*)
8. Interior carotid artery and plexus nerves (*Arteri... terior caro... plexus nerve...*)
9. HYPOPHYSIS (*Hypophysi... cerebri*)
10. Straight sinus (*Sinus rect...*)
11. Ophthalmic vein (*Vena optha...*)
12. Cavernous sinus (*Sinus cavernos...*)
13. Transverse sinus (*Sinus transve...*)
14. Superior petrosal... (*Sinus petrosus... superior*)
15. Occipital sinus (*Sinus occipital...*)
16. Inferior petrosal... (*Sinus petrosus... inferior*)
17. Superior cervical ganglion (*Gangli... cervicale super...*)
18. Internal jugular (*Vena jugular... interna*)
19. Vagus nerve (*Nervus vagus...*)
20. Internal carotid (*Arteria carot... interna*)
21. External carotid artery (*Arteria carotis extern...*)
22. Superior laryngeal nerve (*Nervus laryngealis superior*)
23. Superior thyroid vessels (*... superiora thyreoidea*)
24. Common carotid artery (*Arteria carotis comm...*)
25. THYROID (*Glans thyre...*)
26. Middle and inferior thyroid veins (*Venae thyreoidea... mediales et inferiores*)
27. Thoracic duct (*Ductus thoracicus*)
28. Thyroid axis (*Axis thyr...*)
29. Subclavian artery and vein (*Arteria et vena subcla...*)
30. THYMUS (*Thymus*)
31. Internal thoracic artery and vein (*A. et ... thoracicae internae*)
32. Vagus nerve (*Nervus...*)
33. Superior vena cava (*Vena cava superio...*)
34. Arch of aorta (*Arcus a...*)
35. Pulmonary artery (*Arteria pulmonaria*)
36. Pulmonary veins (*Venae pulmonariae*)
37. Heart (*Cor*)   38. Liver
39. Hepatic nerves (*Nervi hepatici*)
40. Inferior vena cava (*Vena cava inferior*)
41. Oesophagus (*Oesophag...*)
42. Portal vein (*Vena port...*)

LOCATIONS OF ENDOCRINE GLANDS

(CONTINUED ON NEXT PAGE)

43. ADRENALS (Suprarenal glands)
    (*Glandulae suprarenales*)
44. Spleen (*Lien*)
45. Splenic artery and vessels
    (*A. et Vv. lienales accessoriae*)
46. Coeliac ganglion
    (*Ganglion coeliacum*)
47. Suprarenal artery and vein
    Arteria et vena suprarenales)
48. Renal artery and vein
    (*Arteria et vena renales*)

49. Common bile duct (*Ductus choledochus communis*)
50. Pancreatic duct
    (*Ductus pancreaticus*)
51. Pancreas (*Pancreas*)
52. Kidney (*Ren*)
53. Superior mesenteric artery and vein. (*Arteria et vena mesentericae superiores*)
54. Vena cava (*Vena cava*)
55. Aorta (*Aorta*)
56. Ovarian artery, vein and nerves (*Arteria, vena et nervi ovarii*)

57. Testicular artery and vein and nerves to testis
    (*A. et V. testiculares et nervi testiculares*)
58. Internal iliac artery and vein (*A. et V. interiores*)
59. Fallopian tube
    (*Tuba uterina*)
60. OVARY (*Ovarium*)
61. Uterus (*Uterus*)
62. Seminal duct
    (*Ductus deferens*)
63. Uterine artery and vein
    (*A. et V uteri*)
64. Epididymis (*Epididymis*)
65. TESTIS (*Testis*)

HYPOPHYSIS

1. Stalk (*Infundibulum*)
2. Posterior lobe
   (*Lobus posterior*)
3. Anterior lobe
   (*Lobus anterior*)
4. Third ventricle
   (*Ventriculus tertius*)
5. Optic chiasm
   (*Chiasma optica*)

TOP VIEW

SIDE VIEW

X 5

HYPOPHYSIS

The PITUITARY gland (HYPOPHYSIS), measuring about one cm. in diameter, exerts a controlling influence on other endocrine structures. Its two lobes are situated behind the orbits and below the base of the brain, with which it is connected by means of the pituitary stalk. It is enclosed by the "half shell" of the sella turcica of the sphenoid bone. This dual organ is derived from two sources: the anterior lobe from the lining of the embryonic mouth, and the posterior lobe from nerve cells of the third ventricle of the brain.

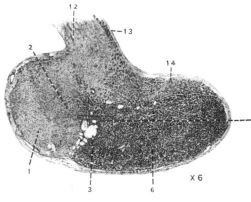

X 6

SAGITTAL SECTION

1. Posterior lobe *(Lobus posterior)*
2. Basophil cells of posterior lobe
3. Cyst *(Cystis)*
4. Intermediate lobe
    (Pars intermedia)
5. Intraglandular cleft *(Fissura)*
6. Anterior lobe *(Lobus anterior)*
7. Acidophil cells
8. Chromophobe cells
9. Basophil cells
10. Connective tissue
11. Blood vessel
12. Stalk
13. Cells of stalk
14. Capsule *(Capsula)*

HYPOPHYSIS

X 265

The anterior lobe comprises the tuberal and distal parts of the pituitary. The cells of this lobe are arranged in columns and consist of two types: chromophil cells (acidophil and basophil) containing pigment granules; and chromophobe cells, or "reserve cells." The names of the hormones secreted describe their principal functions. For example, the adrenocorticotrophic hormone (ACTH) increases the activity of the cortex of the adrenal gland.

The following seven pituitary hormones have been identified: (1) The growth hormone (somatotrophin) increases the amount of protein and stimulates ossification of long bones. (2) The thyroid-stimulating hormone (TSH) increases the production of the thyroid hormone and raises the rate at which this hormone is discharged into the blood stream. (3) The adrenocorticotrophic hormone (ACTH) stimulates the cortex of the adrenal gland to increase the production of glucocorticoids. Physical and psychic stress increase the output of ACTH. (4) The follicle-stimulating hormone (FSH) influences the maturation of ova and spermatozoa. (5) The interstitial-cell-stimulating hormone (ICSH) increases the sex hormone secretions of the body. In females, ICSH stimulates the ovaries to increase secretion of sex hormones (estrogen and progesterone) and is necessary for the early maturation of ova; in males, it stimulates the interstitial cells of the testes to increase their output of the male sex hormone. (6) Prolactin stimulates growth of breast tissue and maintains milk production. (7) Melanocyte-stimulating hormones (MSH) play a role in skin pigmentation.

The posterior lobe of the pituitary comprises the intermediate and neural parts and the stalk (infundibulum) which connects the gland with the base of the third ventricle of the brain. It is principally a storage organ for hormones secreted by nuclei of the adjoining section of the brain, the hypothalamus. The cells (pituicytes) are irregular in shape, imbedded in a network formed by nerve fibers and capillaries. The nerve cells and nerve fibers of the nuclei are filled with droplets of hormones. Two of these hormones have been identified: the antidiuretic hormone and oxytocin. The antidiuretic hormone (ADH) reduces the output of urine by increasing the reabsorption of water by the kidney tubules. This hormone also causes constriction of the coronary arteries in the heart, which lowers the power of the heart muscle and thus reduces cardiac output. Blood pressure may rise because of the arterial constriction. (This hormone is therefore also called vasopressin, pitressin, or pituitrin.) Oxytocin produces powerful contraction of the uterus and causes ejection of milk by stimulating the muscles of the nipple.

150

PINEAL BODY

The PINEAL body lies above the third ventricle and is attached to the mid-brain by the habenular and posterior commissures. It is somewhat smaller than the pituitary gland. Some evidence suggests that it is a vestigial organ, the remnant of a third eye. The pineal body is surrounded by the pia mater except at its points of attachment. Fibrous septa and vessels proceeding from the pia mater divide the gland into chords of cells. The chief or specific cells have a pale nucleus and elongated cytoplasmic branches which terminate with swollen ends—claviform processes. The pineal body reaches its maximum size in children. In adults increasing numbers of neuroglial cells identical with the supporting cells of the brain are present. Laminated bodies of calcium salts, so-called brain sand, appear. The endocrine function of the pineal body has not been established. Tumors of the pineal in prepubertal children produce accelerated sexual development.

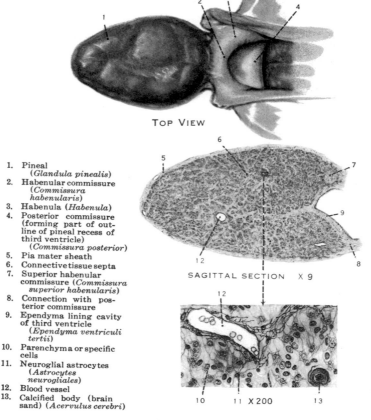

TOP VIEW

1. Pineal (*Glandula pinealis*)
2. Habenular commissure (*Commissura habenularis*)
3. Habenula (*Habenula*)
4. Posterior commissure (forming part of outline of pineal recess of third ventricle) (*Commissura posterior*)
5. Pia mater sheath
6. Connective tissue septa
7. Superior habenular commissure (*Commissura superior habenularis*)
8. Connection with posterior commissure
9. Ependyma lining cavity of third ventricle (*Ependyma ventriculi tertii*)
10. Parenchyma or specific cells
11. Neuroglial astrocytes (*Astrocytes neurogliales*)
12. Blood vessel
13. Calcified body (brain sand) (*Acervulus cerebri*)

SAGITTAL SECTION X 9

X 200

PINEAL

THYROID

The THYROID gland is a highly vascular organ composed of two lateral lobes connected by a narrow strip of tissue or "isthmus." It is situated in the neck, immediately over the trachea. The functioning unit of the gland is the thyroid follicle with varying secretory activity. The cells are usually cuboidal and rest directly on the interfollicular connective tissue which contains blood and lymph capillaries. The normal follicle is moderately distended with colloidal substance that is high in iodine content. (Nearly all of the iodine in the body is found in the thyroid.) From the tissue of the gland, three compounds containing iodine have been extracted: iodothyroglobulin, diodothyrosine, and thyroxin. The thyroid hormone increases the rate of oxidation in the body (heat production) and of the sugar metabolism. It also promotes growth, ossification of bones, and development of teeth, and stimulates the nervous system, the adrenals, and the gonads.

PARATHYROIDS

The PARATHYROID glands are four small, pear-shaped bodies behind the thyroid gland. They are composed of dense masses of epithelial cells resembling in size and shape those of the anterior pituitary lobe. The gland contains small amounts of connective tissue and is highly vascular. The principal cells have fairly large nuclei and clear, pale cytoplasm. They are considered the functioning cells of the gland which secrete the *parathyroid hormone*. Other cells, which stain more deeply and

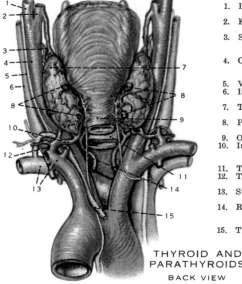

1. Internal carotid artery (*Arteria carotis interna*)
2. External carotid artery (*Arteria carotis externa*)
3. Superior thyroid vessels (*Vascula thyreoidea superiora*)
4. Common carotid artery (*Arteria carotis communis*)
5. Vagus nerve (*Nervus vagus*)
6. Internal jugular vein (*Vena jugularis interna*)
7. Thyroid gland (*Glans thyreoidea*)
8. Parathyroids (*Glandulae parathyreoideae*)
9. Oesophagus (*Oesophagus*)
10. Inferior thyroid vessels (*Vascula thyreoidea inferiora*)
11. Trachea (*Trachea*)
12. Thyroid axis (*Axis thyreoideus*)
13. Subclavian artery and vein (*A. et V. subclaviales*)
14. Recurrent laryngeal nerves (*Nervi laryngeales recurrentes*)
15. Thoracic duct (*Ductus thoracicus*)

THYROID AND PARATHYROIDS
BACK VIEW

which contain oxyphilic granules in the cytoplasm, are scattered in the gland substance. Occasionally, these oxyphil cells form small *acini* with colloid-like secretion. By controlling the amount of calcium and phosphorus in the blood, the parathyroid hormone regulates the metabolism of bones and maintains normal functioning of the nerves and the muscles, including the heart.

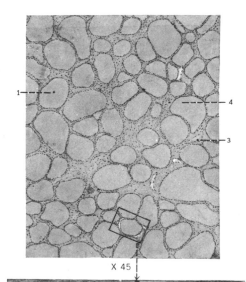

X 45

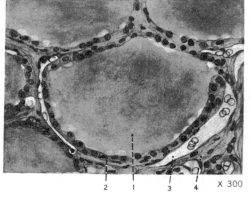

X 300

1. Follicle containing colloid
2. Cuboidal follicular epithelium
3. Blood vessel
4. Interfollicular connective tissue

THYROID

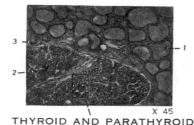

1. Thyroid gland
2. Parathyroid gland
3. Connective tissue

X 45

THYROID AND PARATHYROID

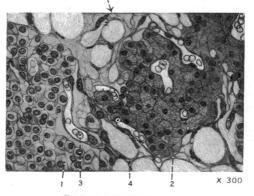

X 300

PARATHYROID

1. Principal cells (pale and clear cytoplasm, large nuclei)
2. Oxyphil cells (larger cells, smaller nuclei)
3. Blood sinus
4. Connective tissue

THYMUS

The THYMUS is a fairly large gland situated deep in the neck, and decreases in size after the period of puberty. The gland is composed of two main lobes, each divided into a number of lobules, separated by dense connective tissue. Each lobule contains a peripheral dense portion or cortex and a more lightly staining central portion or medulla. The cortex is composed of tightly packed lymphocytes with small dense nuclei and little cytoplasm. Passing toward the medulla, the number of lymphocytes decreases and larger, paler cells—the reticular epithelial cells—are found. Scattered throughout the medulla are the whorls of elongated epithelial cells known as Hassall's corpuscles. These often degenerate and become hyalinized at the center. The medulla of the thymus is more vascular than the cortex. In adults the lymphoid cortex becomes thin and the epithelial cells of the medulla are compressed and finally replaced by fat.

The endocrine functions of the thymus are unknown. Some workers believe that it secretes a hormone which hastens sexual maturity.

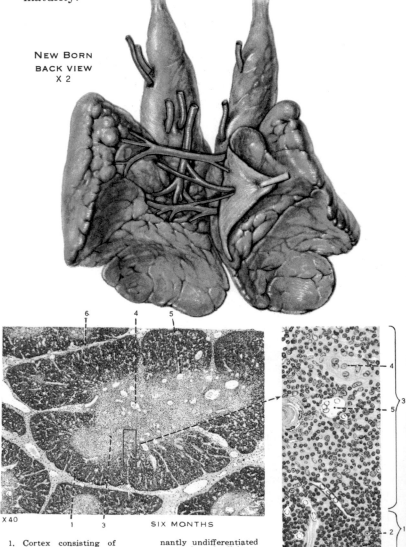

NEW BORN
BACK VIEW
X 2

X 40

SIX MONTHS

1. Cortex consisting of densely packed masses of lymphocytes
2. Undifferentiated mesenchymal cells (reticular cells)
3. Medulla (predomi-
nantly undifferentiated mesenchymal cells)
4. Hassall's corpuscle (epithelial cells)
5. Blood vessel
6. Interlobular connective tissue

X 300

THYMUS

THE ADRENAL GLANDS

The two adrenal (suprarenal) glands are small cup-shaped flat bodies situated above and in front of the upper pole of each kidney. The cut surface of the adrenal shows that the outer three-fourths forms the cortex (rind). This portion is deep yellow, whereas the central core, the medulla, is dark red. The cortex is arranged in three layers: zona glomerulosa; zona fasciculata; and zona reticularis. (A fourth layer exists in infants until the end of the first year.) The cells of the first layer—the narrow, outer zone—form clusters; their nuclei stain deeply. The cells in the second layer, which is the broadest, are arranged in radial bands. The cells in the third layer form a loose, highly vascular network. Some of the latter cells contain a dark pigment. The third layer is in close contact with the core of the gland, the medulla. The medullary cells contain small, brown granules. Since these cells are readily stained by chromates, they are termed *chromaffin cells.*

The adrenal cortex is essential to life. Its hormones, which belong to the chemical class known as steroids, provide vital regulatory functions. There are two corticosteroids: gulcocorticoids ("sugar" hormones); and mineralocorticoids ("salt" hormones). The principal function of the glucocorticoids is to regulate metabolism, particularly of glucose (sugar). The functions of the mineralocorticoids are to maintain the balance between the various minerals, especially sodium and potassium, and to regulate the water content of the body. They also exert important influences on inflammatory and allergic reactions throughout the body. It should be noted that, in addition to the foregoing, the cortex secretes three groups of sex hormones

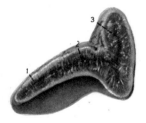
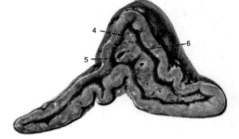

NEW BORN
CROSS SECTION
X 2

ADULT
CROSS SECTION
X 2

1. True cortex
   (*Substantia corticalis*)
2. Androgenic (embryonic) zone
3. Medulla
   (*Substantia medullaris*)

4. Cortex (*Substantia corticalis*)
5. Reticular zone of cortex
   (*Zona reticularis corticis*)
6. Medulla
   (*Substantia medullaris*)

ADRENAL

whose actions are apparently identical with those of the hormones furnished by the testes and ovaries, respectively.

The medulla secretes epinephrine (adrenalin) and norepinephrine (noradrenalin). These hormones increase the rate and power of the heart and raise the blood pressure by constricting blood vessels. They also relax smooth muscle which constricts the bronchial tubes; this action accounts for the efficacy of adrenalin in allergies, including asthma.

The two component sections of the adrenal gland (the cortex and the medulla) are of different origin. They are derived, respectively, from the mesoderm and from the ectoderm, two of the three layers of the embryo. Closely related anatomically, they perform interlocking functions whereby the body reacts to stress, as in times of injury, infection, temperature extremes, or psychic strain (the stress reaction). The body tries to step up its defense mechanisms by increasing the secretion of both cortical hormones and epinephrine. It is an old clinical observation that fatigue lowers the defenses against infection. The concept of the stress reaction, involving the adrenal glands, has provided insight into the mechanism (and identification of its site) whereby the body attempts to cope with fatigue and stress.

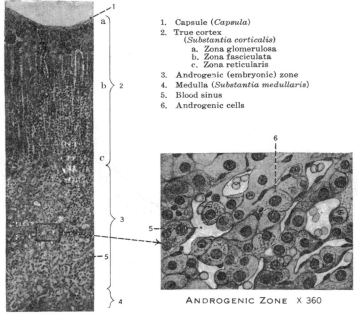

1. Capsule (*Capsula*)
2. True cortex
   (*Substantia corticalis*)
   a. Zona glomerulosa
   b. Zona fasciculata
   c. Zona reticularis
3. Androgenic (embryonic) zone
4. Medulla (*Substantia medullaris*)
5. Blood sinus
6. Androgenic cells

X 45

ANDROGENIC ZONE X 360

ADRENAL
NEW BORN

157

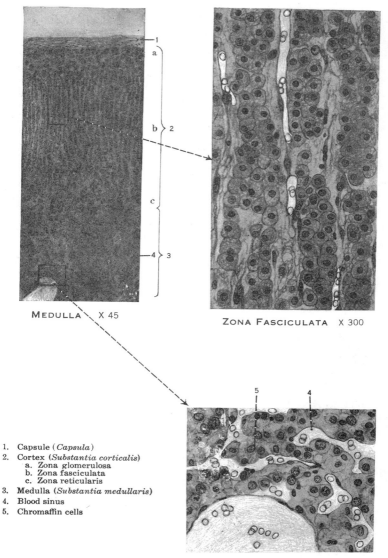

MEDULLA X 45

ZONA FASCICULATA X 300

1. Capsule (*Capsula*)
2. Cortex (*Substantia corticalis*)
   a. Zona glomerulosa
   b. Zona fasciculata
   c. Zona reticularis
3. Medulla (*Substantia medullaris*)
4. Blood sinus
5. Chromaffin cells

MEDULLA X 300

ADRENAL
ADULT

THE PANCREAS

The pancreas is a narrow gland situated behind the stomach between the loop of the duodenum on the right and the spleen on the left. The bulk of the organ is composed of acinous (grape-like) cells which produce various digestive juices. These external (exocrine) secretions are discharged into the duodenum through a duct. Scattered among the acini are the islets of Langerhans, consisting of alpha cells (with fine acidophil granules) and the more numerous beta cells (with alcohol-soluble granules). The alpha cells produce glucagon, while the beta cells produce insulin. Passing directly into the blood vessels, these two hormones constitute the internal (endocrine) secretion of the pancreas. Insulin regulates carbohydrate metabolism and is essential to life. Glucagon has functions which are partly antagonistic and partly complementary to insulin. Failure of the pancreas to secrete adequate insulin causes elevation of the blood sugar level (hyperglycemia), i.e., diabetes mellitus, characterized by loss of weight, profuse urination, and excessive thirst. Excessive secretion of insulin by the pancreas (or an inadequate supply of sugar) causes a low blood sugar level, a condition characterized by nervousness, sweating, extreme hunger, and fatigue.

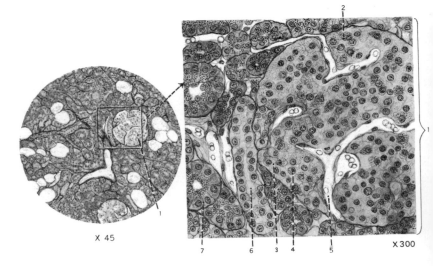

X 45

X 300

1. Islet of Langerhans
2. A Cells (large granules)
3. B Cells (medium sized granules)
4. D Cells (small granules)
5. Blood vessel
6. Pancreatic duct (*Ductus pancreaticus*)
7. Pancreatic acinar cells containing zymogen granules

PANCREAS

OVARY

The OVARIES are paired organs which lie in the abdominal cavity at either end of the broad ligament. They are covered by germinal epithelium and contain dense interstitial connective tissue. During development the germinal epithelium extends into the interstitial tissue, and from these downgrowing processes are developed the ovarian follicles which contain the *female germ cells* or *ova*. The mature follicles rupture through the surface of the ovary and discharge their eggs. From the remains of the ruptured follicle, the corpus luteum develops.

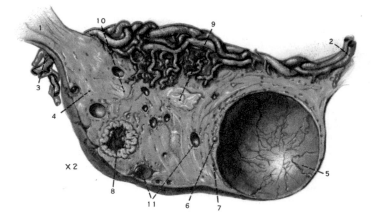

1. Ovarian ligament
   (*Ligamentum ovarii*)
2. Ovarian artery and vein
   (*Arteria et vena ovarii*)
3. Uterine artery and vein
   (*Arteria et vena uteri*)
4. Ovarian stroma
   (*Stroma ovarii*)
5. Graafian follicle
   Folliculus Graafii
6. Ovum (*Ovum*)
7. Theca interna and externa
   (*Theca interna et externa*)
8. Corpus luteum (of menstruation, regressing)
9. Corpus luteum (later stage of regression)
10. Corpus albicans (complete regression)
11. Developing follicles
12. True lutein layer
13. Central necrosis and scarring

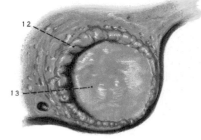

X 2 CORPUS LUTEUM
LATE PREGNANCY
CROSS SECTION

OVARY
ADULT
CROSS SECTION

The ovarian follicles in young individuals are small and numerous at the periphery and are called primary follicles. The center of the follicle is occupied by a large ovum which has a refractile nucleus and a conspicuous nucleolus and a large amount of clear cytoplasm. It is surrounded in turn by a layer of follicular cells, and the ovarian connective tissue. With maturity there is growth in the ovum, follicular cells, and adjacent connective tissue. The follicular cells, which are columnar or polyhedral in shape, multiply rapidly as the follicle increases in size; fluid accumulates and presses the follicular cells to the periphery. The ovum remains embedded in a solid mass of follicular cells, the DISCUS PROLIGERUS; the layer of cells in contact with the ovum being known as the CORONA RADIATA.

The connective tissue surrounding the follicular epithelium differentiates into two surrounding layers, the THECA INTERNA and THECA EXTERNA. The theca interna is highly vascular and epitheloid in appearance. The theca externa is composed of dense circularly arranged fusiform cells with fibres.

The fully differentiated follicular cells are termed GRANULOSA CELLS and secrete the ovarian hormone *oestrin*. This hormone produces rapid growth in the endometrial lining of the uterus and in the uterine musculature, and causes cornification in the squamous cells of the vagina and cervix. It also stimulates the development of the milk ducts and periductal connective tissue in the mammary gland. Tumors of granulosa cells produce premature sexual development in young girls and in elderly women may bring about the return of uterine bleeding.

After discharge of the ovum from the ripened follicle about the mid period of the menstrual cycle, the granulosa cells and the cells of the theca interna rapidly enlarge. The enlarged follicular cells with pale cytoplasm become the true corpus luteum cells (follicular lutein cells) and the cells of the theca interna become theca lutein cells. The theca lutein or paralutein cells are smaller but similar to the lutein cells. This corpus luteum of menstruation persists until the onset of menstruation when hemorrhage and involutional changes appear.

If the recently discharged ovum is fertilized the corpus luteum of menstruation becomes the corpus luteum of pregnancy, the lutein cells continuing to enlarge, reaching their maximum size at the mid period of pregnancy when involution begins.

The hormone of the corpus luteum, *progesterone*, has been isolated and prepared synthetically. It produces secretory changes in the uterine endometrium, inhibits uterine contractility and is used therapeutically in cases of threatened abortion.

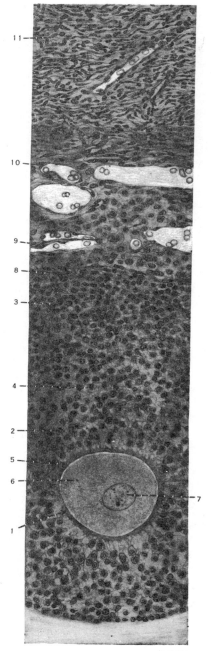

1. Ovum (*Ovum*)
2. Corona radiata (epithelial follicular cells) (*Corona radiata*)
3. Discus proligerus (*Discus proligerus*)
4. Mitosis in follicular cell (*Mitosis*)
5. Zona pellucida (*Zona pellucida*)
6. Protoplasm of ovum
7. Nucleus (germinal vesicle) with nucleolus (germinal spot)
8. Basement membrane
9. Theca interna with abundant blood vessels Corpus luteum of menstruation (or pregnancy) (*Theca interna*)
10. Theca externa fewer blood vessels (*Theca externa*)
11. Ovarian stroma (*Stroma ovarii*)

OVARY

THROUGH GRAAFIAN FOLLICLE
AND OVARIAN TISSUE

X 250

162

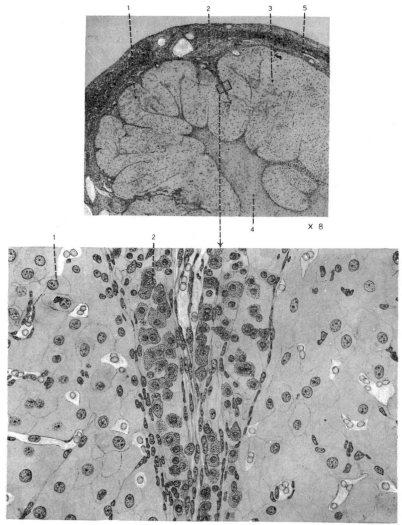

X 8

X 250

1. True lutein cells
2. Paralutein cells
3. Capillaries
4. Central scarring
5. Compressed ovarian stroma about corpus luteum

CORPUS LUTEUM
PREGNANCY

TESTIS

The TESTES contain coils of secreting seminiferous tubules, in which the spermatozoa are formed. These tubules are arranged in lobules which converge toward a hilum, the RETE TESTIS. From here the spermatozoa pass into a coiled mass of excretory ducts, the EPIDIDYMIS, whence they leave the testis via the VAS DEFERENS.

The adult convoluted seminiferous tubules are lined with spermatogenic cells and by supporting elements, the SERTOLI CELLS. The Sertoli cells have vesicular nuclei, with a dense nucleolus, and an irregular reticular cytoplasm. These cells do not undergo active division under normal conditions.

The spermatogenic cells are continually dividing in the normal adult, and give rise to a series of cell forms terminating with the formation of MOTILE SPERMATOZOA. The process is as follows: The spermatogenic cells, with large dust-like nuclei, lie near the basement membrane of the seminiferous tubule. These cells undergo mitotic division and approach the lumen of the tubule. The recently divided cells nearest the lumen are known as PRIMARY SPERMATOCYTES. These primary spermatocytes divide into new cells, the secondary spermatocytes, which again divide to give rise to smaller cells with dense nuclei, the SPERMATIDS. The spermatids are the last generation of the spermatogenic cells. The spermatids develop a spearheaded nucleus, behind which is a collar of cytoplasm and an elongated tail. These are the spermatozoa which will become motile.

In the connective tissue which separates these seminiferous tubules are found nests of cells, the interstitial cells of Leydig. The interstitial cells are believed to secrete the male sex hormone, *testosterone*. This hormone is responsible for the development of accessory male genital organs. including growth of pubic and body hair and normal sexual behavior. It promotes other metabolic processes; for example, it stimulates the growth of bone, and it causes ossification of the epiphyses when full adult size has been attained. As the production of the hormone decreases with age, sexual functions gradually regress.

164

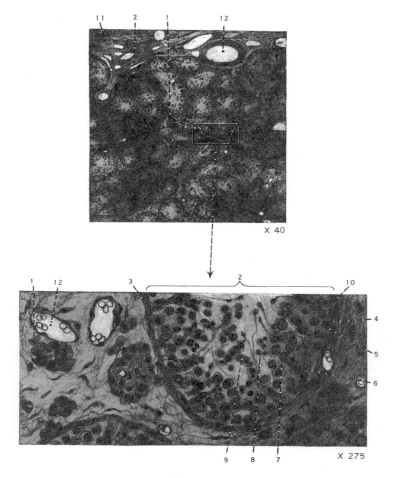

X 40

X 275

ADULT
SHOWING STAGES OF SPERMATOGENESIS

1. Interstitial cells of Leydig
2. Seminiferous tubule
3. Basement membrane
4. Primary spermatocyte
5. Mitotic spermatocyte
6. Spermatogenic cell

7. Secondary sperma-tocyte
8. Spermatids
9. Spermatozoa
10. Sertoli or supporting cell
11. Tunica albuginea
12. Blood vessel

TESTIS

DISORDERS OF THE ENDOCRINE GLANDS

The following are the principal disorders of the pituitary gland: (1) Overproduction of the growth hormone in childhood causes giantism; the individual may grow to eight feet or more. Overproduction in adult life causes acromegaly. characterized by thickening of skin and enlargement of tongue and of bones in the face, lower jaw, hands, and feet. (2) Overproduction of ACTH may cause the adrenal disorder known as Cushing's syndrome. (3) Undersecretion of the growth hormone causes dwarfism, failure of bone growth, and other endocrine defects, including subnormal sexual functions. (4) Simmond's disease is caused by destruction of the adenohypophysis, resulting from hemorrhage during labor or from growth of a tumor. The results are cessation of lactation and of menstruation and deficient functioning of the thyroid and adrenal glands. Administration of thyroid, cortisone, and estrogen have produced good results. (5) Diabetes insipidus results from inadequate secretion of the antidiuretic hormone (ADH), perhaps as the consequence of disease of the neurohypophysis or of the nuclei of the hypothalamus. This condition is characterized by passage of large quantities of dilute urine, possibly in excess of five liters daily. The resulting loss of water causes extreme thirst (polydipsia). If the hormonal deficiency is caused by a tumor, surgical removal or X-ray treatment may be beneficial. In many cases, administration of ADH produces substantial improvement. (6) Hypothalamic-pituitary disorders may arise from tumors affecting the hypothalamus without actually involving the pituitary gland. On account of the close proximity of these structures, pressure may cause hormonal disturbances in the pituitary. Common manifestations are sexual abnormalities, either in the form of hypogonadism (deficiency) or of hypergonadism (excess), with the latter, in children, leading to precocious puberty.

The most common disorders of the thyroid gland are as follows: (1) Hyperthyroidism, by overproducing thyroxin, abnormally increases the functions of the gland. Symptoms include loss of weight, nervousness, and rapid heart action. The eyes may protrude (exophthalmos) as a result of increased amounts of fat and water in the orbits, followed by swelling of the extraocular muscles and growth of fibrous tissue. Subsequent degeneration of these muscles may render the protrusion of the eyes permanent. (2) In hypothyroidism (myxedema) the picture is reversed. Overweight, dryness of the skin, and mental sluggishness become severe, and the cholesterol level of the blood rises. If the thyroid deficiency develops in infancy, cretinism may supervene, characterized by dwarfism and mental retardation. (3) Goiter refers to enlargement of the thyroid gland; the condition is prevalent in areas where the soil and water are deficient in iodine. Excellent results in correcting the foregoing thyroid disorders have been achieved through medicinal and operative procedures.

In overactivity of the parathyroid gland, there is bone destruction, the calcium level of the blood rises, and kidney stones may form. In underactivity, the blood calcium level drops and there is increased excitability of nerves and muscles. The latter condition may progress to tetany. In the early stages of this disorder, there are sensations of stiffness; in the more advanced stages, there are muscular spasms, which may involve the larynx, and general convulsions.

Clinical manifestations of adrenal disorders show great variations as the result of differences in the anatomical locations affected. Addison's disease is an example of depressed functioning of the adrenal cortex. The outstanding features are weakness, pigmentation of the skin, and loss of weight. The isolation of corticosteroids has led to the development of successful treatment. Overactivity of the adrenals, producing excessive secretions, is usually the result of tumor formation. Cushing's syndrome is characterized by marked obesity of the body and face (moon face) without involvement of the limbs. There is considerable elevation of the blood pressure. Female patients develop masculine traits owing to excessive production of male hormones. Favorable results have been obtained by operative procedure. Surgical treatment has also frequently been highly successful in dealing with tumors of the adrenal medulla (pheochromocytoma) which produce elevation of the blood pressure and of the pulse rate.

In diabetes mellitus (see page 158) the administration of insulin and other medications has been effective. Oral treatment has given promising results in selected cases of this disorder. In the reverse condition, hypoglycemia (caused by an excess of insulin), the administration of suitable food is helpful in mild cases. Surgery is necessary if there is a chronic condition caused by tumors involving the pancreatic tissue.

SELECTED BIBLIOGRAPHY

Arey, L. B. *Developmental Anatomy.* 7th ed. Saunders, 1965. Summarizes functional and structural aspects of embryology.

Bloom, W. and Fawcett, D. W. *Textbook of Histology.* 8th ed. Saunders, 1962. A new edition of a popular text. Several chapters have been rewritten and brought up-to-date.

Carlson, A. V. and Johnson, V. *The Machinery of the Body.* 5th ed. Univ. of Chicago, 1961.

Cunningham's *Textbook of Anatomy* (ed. by G. J. Romanes). 10th ed. Oxford, 1964. A standard, authoritative text well adapted to the needs of medical students and physicians.

Evans, F. G. *Stress and Strain in Bones.* Thomas, 1957.

Gifford's *Textbook of Ophthalmology* (ed. by F. H. Adler). 7th ed. Saunders, 1957. Concise, practical information on the anatomy and physiology of the eye.

Gray's *Anatomy* (ed. by C. M. Goss). 27th ed. Lea & Febiger, 1959. The classic text with many new illustrations and discussion of results of recent researches.

Kaplan, E. B. *Functional and Surgical Anatomy of the Hand.* 2nd ed. Lippincott, 1965.

Kleiner, I. S. and Orten, J. M. *Biochemistry,* 6th ed. Mosby, 1962.

Lockhart, R. D. et al. *Anatomy of the Human Body.* Lippincott, 1959.

Morris' *Human Anatomy* (ed. by J. P. Schaeffer). 11th ed. McGraw-Hill, 1953.

Patten, B. M. *Human Embryology.* 2nd ed. McGraw-Hill, 1953.

Ransom, S. W. *The Anatomy of the Nervous System* (ed. by S. L. Clark). 10th ed. Saunders, 1959.

Steen, E. B. and Montagu, M. F. Ashley. *Anatomy and Physiology.* 2 vols. (College Outline Series). Barnes and Noble, 1959.

Wheeler, R. C. *Textbook of Dental Anatomy and Physiology.* 4th ed. Saunders, 1965.

White, J. and Sweet, W. H. *Pain: Its Mechanisms and Neurosurgical Control.* Thomas, 1955.

Williams, R. H. et al. *Textbook of Endocrinology.* 3rd ed. Saunders, 1962.

Wintrobe, M. M. *Clinical Hematology.* 5th ed. Lea & Febiger, 1961. A clinical volume which also analyzes a great deal of basic physiology and biochemistry, including methods of diagnosing and treating diseases of the blood.

Wolff, E. *Anatomy of the Eye and Orbit* (ed. by R. J. Last). 5th ed. Saunders, 1961. A dependable guide to the anatomy of the eye. 438 illustrations.

INDEX
Italics refer to illustrations.

A

Abdomen, *129–132*
  arteries of, 79, 131
  lymph ducts of, 80
  muscles of, 37, 38
  regions of, 2
  veins of, 79
Abdominal aorta, *131*
Abdominal cavity, 2, 89, 105
Abdominal region, 2
Abdominal wall, 38, 105, *120*
Abduction, 31, 33
Abortion, 160
Abscess, 18, 64, 88
Absorption, 89, 93, 97
Accommodation, 67
Acetabulum, 30
Achilles' reflex, 49
Achilles' tendon, 49
Acid-base equilibrium, 99
Acidophil cells, *148*, 149
Acids, amino, 94, 98
  hydrochloric, 93
  nucleic, 94
  uric, 34, 103
Acne, 18
Acromegaly, 165
Acromion (prominence) of scapula, 28
"Adam's apple," 84
Adaptation, 4, 5
Addison's disease, 166
Adduction, 32
Adipose tissue, 10
Adolescence, 115
Adrenal glands, 81, *146, 147, 155–157*
Adrenalin (epinephrine), 156
Afferent neurons, 45, 48, 55
Afterbirth, 114
Albumin in urine, 103
Alcohol, 98
Alimentary canal, 89
Allergy, 18, 42, 73, 83, 155, 156
All-or-none principle, 47
Alveolar ducts, 87
Alveolar glands, 14
Alveolar sacs, 82, 87
Alveoli of lungs, 82, 87
Amines, 95
Amino acids, 94, 98
Amnion, 114, *142*
Ampulla, of ductus deferens, 105
  of rectum, 95
  of semicircular canals, 62, 69
Anabolism, 98
Anal canal, 95
Anatomic position, 1
Anatomy, 1
Androgenic zone, 155, 156
Anemia, 18, 72, 81
Anesthetics, 48
Angina pectoris, 71, 77
Angiology, 1
Angle of rib, 27
Ankle movement, 32
Ankylosis, 32, 34
Anomalies, twinning, 113
Antagonists, 38–39
Anterior, 1
Antibiotics, 88
Antibodies, 72, 73, 81
Antrum, pyloric, 92
Anuria, 103
Anus, 94, 110, 112, *140, 141*
Anvil, 62, 63

Aorta, 75–79, *123, 127, 131, 140*
  abdominal, *131*, 140
Aortic arch, *146*
Apex, of heart, 74
  of lung, 87
Aphasia, 54
Aponeuroses, 138
Apoplexy, 42, 47
Apparatus, lacrimal, 64, 66
Appendicitis, 98
Appendicular skeleton, 21, 22, *118, 119*
Appendix, vermiform, 94, *130*, 133
Aqueous humor, 65, 67
Arachnoid membrane, 27, 54
Arbor vitae, 51
Arc, reflex, 48, *49*
Arch, aortic, *146*
  vertebral, 25
Areola, 111
Areolar tissue, 10
Arm, arteries of, 78, *125, 126*
  bones of, 28, 29, 30, *118, 119*
  circulatory system of, *126*
  muscles, 40, *120, 121*
  nerves of, *122*
  veins of, *126*
Arterial ligament, *127*
Artery (ies), 76–79, *125, 126*
  abdominal, 79, 131
  aortic, 76–79, *125, 127, 131*, 140
  axillary, 78
  basilar, 79
  brachial, 78
  brachiocephalic, 78
  carotid, 77, *126, 128, 146*
  celiac, 79
  central, 67, 71
  cerebral, *128*
  clots in, 73
  common iliac, 79
  coronary, 76, 77
  external iliac, 79
  facial, 78
  femoral, 78, 79
  of head, *128*
  of heart, 78, *125*
  hepatic, 79
  iliac, 79, 102, *147*
  innominate (brachiocephalic), 78
  of lower extremities, 79, *126*
  mesenteric, 79, *126*
  of neck, 79
  ophthalmic, 67
  ovarian, *147*, 159
  popliteal,. 78, 79, *126*
  posterior tibial, 79
  pulmonary, 75, *125*
  radial, *126*
  renal, 79, *126, 147*
  subclavian, 78, *126*
  superior mesenteric, *147*
  testicular, *147*
  tibial, *126*
  ulnar, *126*
  umbilical, 80
  of upper extremities, 78, *126*
  uterine, 102
  vaginal, 102
  vertebral, 79, *126*
Arthritis, 34
Articulations, 19, 31; *see also* Joints
Ascending colon, 89, 94
Asphyxiation, 86
Association areas, 53

170

Bones (Cont.)
upper extremities, 21, 22, *118, 119*
vertebrae, 21, 22, 24, *119, 134*
vomer, 22
wormian, 23
wrist, 21, 22, 28, *119*
zygomatic, 22
Bowlegs, 34
Bowman's capsule, 101
Brachial plexus, 57
Brain, 9, 13, 27, 48, 49, 50–54, 69, 123, 124
abscess, 64
cavities, 54
clots affecting, 73
coverings, 27, 54
fissures, 52
hemispheres, 51–54
injuries, 32, 42, 50, 69
lobes, 52, 53
membranes, 27, 54
meninges, 27, 54
stem, 50
sulci, 52
tracts, 46, 47, 52
ventricles, 54
Breast feeding, 61, 114
Breasts, 104, 111
Breathing, 82–88
Bright's disease, 103
Broad ligament of uterus, 107, 109
Broca's area, 54
Bronchi, 82, 86–87, *132*
Bronchiectasis, 87
Bronchioles, 87
Bronchitis, 87
Buccal cavity, 90
Buccal glands, 95
Bulb, hair, 16
Bulbo-urethral (Cowper's) glands, 105, 106
Bursa, 34
Bursitis, 34

C

Caffeine, 97
Calcium, 19, 34, 103, 150, 152
Calculus, 103
Calyces, 101
Canal, alimentary, 89
anal, 95
cervical, 109, 114
Haversian, 12
inguinal, 38, 105
pyloric, 92
of Schlemm, 65, 71
semicircular, 61, 62
Cancellous bone, 12, 21
Cancer, 6, 16, 18
Canine teeth, 91
Capillaries, blood, 78
Capitulum, 28
Capsule, Glisson's, 96
of hypophysis, *148*
internal, 47
of joint, 32
of kidney, 99, 101
Carbohydrates, 2, 7, 78, 97, 98
Carbon dioxide, 73, 78, 82, 83
Carbon monoxide, 70
Cardiac muscle, 13, 35, 36, 57, 74, 77, *127*
Cardiac orifice, 92
Cardiac spincter of stomach, 92
Cardiac tissue, 13
Caries, 98
Cartilage, 10, 12, 19, 31, 32, 84
Catabolism, 98
Cataract, 71
Caudate lobe, 95, 96
Cavity (ies), abdominal, 89, 105
amniotic, 112

brain, 54
cranial, 27
glenoid, 28
medullary, 21
nasal, 27, 82
of eye, 64, 67
oral, 27
orbital, 27, 68
pericardial, 89
pleural, 89
skull, 27
thoracic, 89
tympanic, 61
Cecum, 89, 94, *129, 130, 133*
Celiac ganglion, 147
Cell(s), 4, 5, 6–9, 112
acidophil, *148*, 149
basophil, *148*, 149
blood, *5*, 72, 74, 80
bone, 12
cartilage, 10–12, 84
chromophobe, *148*, 149
connective tissue, *5*, 9, 10–12
division, *5*, 6, 112
embryonal, *5*
epithelial, *5*, 8, 9
functions, 7–8
glia, 46
granulosa, 160
hyaline, *11*
inclusions, 7
of Leydig, 163, 164
lutein, 160, *162*
malignant, 80
membrane, 7, 82
mitochondria, 7
motile sperm, 163
muscle, *5*, 9, 13
nerve, *5*, 13, *49*
nucleus, 6, 7
organoids, 7
oxyphil, 152, 153
permeability, 7
pituicytes, 149
primary spermatocytes, 163
reproductive, *5*, 6
of Schwann, 46
segmentation, *5*, *108*, 112
Sertoli, 163
sex, 104
spermatids, 163
Cementum, 91
Central lobe, 52
Central nervous system, 43, 49–55
Centrioles, 7
Centrosome, 7
Cerebellum, 50, 51, 69
Cerebrospinal fluid, 54, 62, 72
Cerebrum, 50, 51–54
Cervical plexus, 57
Cervical vertebrae, 22, 24, 25, *119, 134*
Cervix of uterus, 109, *141*, 143, 160
Cesarian operation, 115
Charley horse, 42
Cheeks, 90
Chest, 4, 21, 22, 25, *129–132*
Chiasma, optic, 51
Childbirth, 110, 114, *143*
Childhood, 114
Cholesterol, 94, 96
Choline, 78
Chorea, 54
Chorioid (choroid) of eye, 64
Chorion, 112
Chromatin, 6
Chromonemata, 6
Chromophobe cells, *148*, 149
Chromosomes, 6
Chyme, 93, 97